COUNSELING FOR RELAPSE PREVENTION

By Terence T. Gorski and Merlene Miller

D0097097

HERALD HOUSE—INDEPENDENCE PRESS
P.O. Box HH
3225 South Noland Road
Independence, MO 64055

ISBN 0-8309-0367-4

Printed in the United States of America

10   11   12   13   93 92 91 90 89

**Dedicated to Joe Troiani
for friendship and support**

ACKNOWLEDGEMENTS

We want to thank the many people who helped make this book possible: C.C. Nuckols, Teah Sloan, Cleona Guthrie, Vern Forsythe, Gordon Marking, Jan Berry, Lisa Hodges, Merle Guthrie and especially David Miller who contributes in so many ways.

CONTENTS

INTRODUCTION

Relapse is a critical issue facing the alcoholism field today. The process of relapse is often ignored or misunderstood. As a result, many relapse patients are receiving ineffective or inappropriate treatment. Stigmas and stereotypes have inhibited effective work with relapse-prone alcoholics.

On any given day approximately 20% of the private sector treatment beds in the United States are filled with patients who have been treated for alcoholism on at least one previous occasion. The number of relapse patients and the percentage of resources devoted to them will continue to increase until treatment methods are discovered that will allow full recovery.

The cost of relapse is high. Chronic relapse patients will eventually die from alcoholism. In the last year of their lives they will each spend approximately 150 days in a medical or surgical hospital being treated for the medical complications of alcoholism. Prior to that, many thousands of dollars of society's resources will be drained in failed treatment efforts, crime, accidents, and lost production.

Devising low-cost methods of treating the relapse prone has met with very limited success. As the cost of providing direct services is lowered, the standards of care are lowered and there is little impact upon the related societal expenses associated with relapse.

Traditional treatment methods have failed with relapse-prone patients. Repeated exposures to treatment methods that have failed is not the answer. Logic indicates that this will only result in a population of "professional patients" who never attain full recovery for themselves and who complicate the treatment process for other patients.

In spite of the high cost of relapse, the problem has been ignored. Relapsing patients have been passed from one network of care to another. The treatment failures from the private treatment sector eventually become the problems of the public treatment sector. These failures become the problems of the courts and law enforcement agencies.

Who are the relapse prone, and why do they relapse? Are they the skid row derelicts who have no choice but to drink? Are they the people who have been coerced into treatment but have no self-motivation to recover? Are they the persons assaulted by major situational crisis during recovery? Or are they, perhaps, the alcoholics that haven't "hit bottom" yet, the ones with minimal problems who cannot believe they are alcoholic because they aren't sick enough yet to fit the stereotype?

Many of the persons in these categories do relapse. But many recover. For some, recovery means following the simple program as outlined by Alcoholics Anonymous. For others, recovery becomes possible through the use of AA in combination with professional counseling. But for about 40% of all persons attempting to recover from alcoholism, recovery is elusive. They relapse in spite of their best efforts while skilled treatment professionals stand by helpless because traditional approaches to counseling and treatment simply don't work.

Often professionals don't deal well with helplessness.

Instead of acknowledging the limits of our ability to help and making a commitment to grow beyond those limits, we begin to blame. "He just wasn't ready." "He wasn't motivated." "He got drunk because he stopped going to meetings." "If he had done what I told him, he wouldn't have got into trouble."

The relapse prone are truly among our most desperate clients because they are caught in a trap of misunderstanding. They fail to recover in spite of their best efforts, and when the relapse takes its toll, they blame themselves. When they seek renewed treatment, they often feel the anger and misunderstanding of the therapist. The professionals often blame them for relapsing. This compounds the guilt and sense of helplessness and reinforces the tendency to relapse.

Relapse-prone patients suffer from alcoholism in its most severe form. Not only are the alcohol-based symptoms of that disease disruptive to their lifestyle, the sobriety-based symptoms rob them of judgment and behavioral control and eventually destabilize all areas of life. At the end of this process, they find themselves facing destructive alternatives — suicide, insanity, physical or emotional collapse, or drinking. Faced with these limited choices, many opt for the sanest choice, drinking again.

As our treatment centers are becoming more effective in convincing patients they cannot safely drink, we find many who stay painfully abstinent and attempt to battle this destructive process. Many of them collapse physically from excessive stress, have emotional breakdowns, or commit suicide because they can perceive no other way out.

Counseling For Relapse Prevention

The relapse prone are not confined to the skid row regions, the mental hospitals, the ranks of the poor, or the category of "unmotivated." Just as there is a stigma placed upon the actively drinking alcoholic, there is also a stigma placed upon the relapse-prone person. This stigma must be removed before successful interventions can be found for those who relapse.

Alcoholism is a disease that has two cutting edges. The first attacks while the person is still drinking. This is the obvious and self-evident side of the disease. What is becoming increasingly clear is that there is a second cutting edge to this illness. There is a part of this disease that extends into sobriety and takes a vicious toll on many individuals attempting to recover. This sobriety-based edge of the disease is as powerful and destructive as the alcohol-based edge. The alcoholic is even more helpless in face of it because it is generally misunderstood and unrecognized by both the alcoholic and the treatment professional.

Although our understanding of relapse is limited, a substantial volume of research is emerging which can form the basis of an applied technology for relapse prevention. It is becoming apparent that effectiveness with the relapse patient can be significantly improved. The widespread implementation of relapse prevention technologies can contribute to the reversal of the current alcoholism epidemic.

The first step in interrupting the relapse process is interrupting stigma-oriented thinking. Relapse is part of the disease of alcoholism. It is a free-standing syndrome, such a powerful force in the lives of some that no matter how hard they try and no matter what type of treatment they use, they are powerless to combat it. The relapsers do not will it, and it is stronger in some than in others.

We must stop blaming our patients for relapsing. We must recognize that they are being victimized in sobriety by the same disease that cripples them while drinking. It is important to recognize that loss of control happens before drinking occurs. Early intervention is, therefore, the mandate. As soon as patients get sober, they should be educated about the common warning signs of relapse. A regular and routine part of all counseling should be a review of relapse warning signs and the development of intervention strategies should any of the warning signs become evident.

The relapse patient needs to develop a written list of relapse warning signs after reviewing the known warning signs of relapse. The development of this list of relapse warning signs should occur with the consultation of a knowledgeable alcoholism counselor, the entire family, and the AA sponsor. All persons concerned should be involved in recognizing the indicators that the patient is in trouble and losing control. Every family member should know how to intervene if the alcoholic exhibits signs of loss of control of judgment or behavior even before drinking.

Before a recovering person is in trouble he should design a strategy by which family, friends, treatment personnel, and AA members can be most helpful in interrupting the potential or actual relapse. A recovering person should spell out the game plan that can defeat his denial. He should create rules of the game by which he wants others to play should a relapse occur.

The growing field of intervention technology is

offering hope in the creation of new techniques that will interrupt the relapse process. It is being demonstrated that with effective relapse prevention planning and with early intervention, many relapses can be avoided.

There is more hope for the future because more professionals are becoming concerned and involved. And these professionals are fighting for the advancement of research into the effective diagnosis and treatment of the sobriety-based symptoms of alcoholism.

This book is being written as part of a national offensive against relapse which was initiated by Alcoholism Systems Associates (ASA) of Hazel Crest, Illinois in January of 1982. The objective of this offensive is to bring vital new information about relapse, its treatment and prevention to the professional counseling community and the recovering alcoholics who are struggling with their recovery.

Relapse prevention is not an easy task. It requires a competent counselor who has been trained in relapse prevention technology. This counselor must be able to diagnose alcoholism effectively, support the patient through the typical periods of normal recovery, and identify and treat the factors that complicate the recovery process. He must also be able to work with the patient to facilitate development of a personality style that is conducive to long-term and comfortable sobriety. Finally, the counselor must be able to recognize the early warning signs of relapse itself and be skilled in initiating an individualized relapse prevention plan that involves the patient and the family.

As is usually the case, we learn more from attempting

to treat our most difficult cases than we ever learn from the less difficult ones. It is for this reason that an intensive commitment is being made to learn how to treat the relapse patient more effectively. The ultimate success of the alcoholism treatment profession depends upon our ability to do just that.

This book has been designed to present to you an overview of the theory and research pertaining to relapse in the alcoholic. It is further designed to describe a practical method of treating the relapse patient that is compatible with the principles and practices of both Alcoholics Anonymous and professional alcoholism treatment.

Part One

RELAPSE

THE RELAPSE DYNAMIC

Relapse among alcoholics is common. Many, if not most, return to the use of alcohol at least once after making an honest commitment to sobriety and to pursuing a structured recovery program. About 40% of all alcoholics who initiate treatment that involves both AA and professional alcoholism counseling will find themselves hopelessly and inevitably drawn into the ranks of chronic recidivism. This will occur in spite of their best conscious efforts at sobriety.

While some symptoms of alcoholism are triggered by drinking, other symptoms are triggered by abstinence. These sobriety-based symptoms often strike in the dark. A strange set of complex physical, psychological, and spiritual drives becomes activated and forms a slow but inevitable progression. The victims lose control of their thought processes, judgment, and emotional reactions. Eventually they lose control of all areas of life.

Where does the progression end? For many it ends in a return to alcohol use. But for those who have learned their lessons well — for those who have learned that they cannot drink, no matter what the price — the relapse process can end in death. Every day sober alcoholics commit suicide, die of stress-related illnesses, or kill themselves and others in unnecessary accidents while sober. What's the cause of many of these deaths? The answer is simple but difficult to believe. The cause is the relapse dynamic.

In 1973 a survey was completed of 118 alcoholics who had all been treated in 21- or 28-day rehabilitation programs for alcoholism. All had made a commitment to ongoing sobriety supported by a structured recovery program that involved both Alcoholics Anonymous and professional counseling, and all 118 persons later returned to the uncontrolled use of alcohol. The purpose of the study was to discover what went wrong, to find the cause of relapse.

The results of this study were impressive. It was discovered that there are progressive and predictable warning signs that occur in most alcoholics prior to the time they start to drink. Thirty-seven predictable warning signs were identified and the warning signs seemed to appear in a general progressive order.

This research brought new hope for the recovering alcoholic. If there are predictable warning signs that precede the use of alcohol, perhaps alcoholics and their counselors can recognize these warning signs and intervene before the alcoholic takes the first drink.

Subsequent clinical studies with relapse-prone persons indicated that most of these persons dropped out of treatment before relapse. As a matter of fact, it is a commonly held misconception that the cause of the relapse is discontinuing treatment. A further question must be asked. *What is it that motivates the patient to drop out of treatment?*

The answer leads us back to the hidden sobriety-based symptoms of alcoholism. Something is activated within these people that creates a powerful drive that pulls them away from their structured recovery program. So perhaps the warning signs are not as useful as they first appeared. If the person is not in treatment when the warning signs are noticed, how can the relapse be prevented?

In further clinical work, it was discovered that once the relapse symptoms are activated there is a *progression* of loss of control over thought process, emotional process, and judgment. The symptoms build, grow, and progress. There are many subtle warning signs and many changes in thought process, emotional process, and personality that occur before loss of control.

There is a mistaken belief that relapse only involves the act of taking a drink or using drugs. Relapse is the progressive process that creates the overwhelming need for alcohol. It is this progression that we call the relapse dynamic.

Intervention is possible before the more overt warning signs are obvious. But by the time patients are showing definite signs that they are going to relapse, intervention is generally difficult because they have already lost control of their judgment and their behavior. Even if the warning signs are brought to their attention, it is highly unlikely that they can exert sufficient control over themselves to take the steps necessary to intervene.

It becomes apparent, then, that it is impossible to separate relapse from recovery. As cold is the absence of heat or as darkness the absence of light, relapse is the absence of recovery. To understand how alcoholics relapse we must understand how they recover. Recovery and relapse are two sides of the same coin. We cannot simply look at relapse warning signs. We must look at the other side of the coin and determine what recovery deficits are indicated by the warning signs. Relapse prevention must begin with the initial phase of recovery.

The relapse dynamic is often thought to be volitional or

under the conscious control of the relapsing person. Studies have shown that these persons are generally not consciously aware of the early warning signs of their relapse. In most research interviews and clinical treatment sessions conducted after the relapse, patients can see with hindsight the process that led them to feel they had no choice but to drink. But most indicated that at the time they were unaware that these problems were building and growing. In short, the warning signs of relapse develop on an unconscious level. The patient blocks them from conscious awareness and doesn't know that they are occurring.

It was discovered quite by accident that the simple process of having patients check for the presence of relapse warning signs once a week is highly successful in reducing the rate of relapse. An outpatient research project was designed to test a relapse-prediction questionnaire that listed symptoms that were normally believed to precede relapse. The average relapse rate of that outpatient population was approximately eight percent. Forty-six patients participated in the supervised completion of the relapse-prediction questionnaire on a weekly basis. It was anticipated that four patients would relapse during the three-month study period. This would allow an initial testing of the effectiveness of the questionnaire as a tool for predicting relapse.

During the period of the data collection only two patients returned to drinking, half as many as expected. What reduced the relapse rate in the patients who were completing the questionnaire? There are no definite answers available, but it seems reasonable to believe that it was the use of the questionnaire itself. Since then numerous counselors have reduced the frequency, the duration, and the severity of relapses by challenging recovering alcoholics to do a regular daily inventory to check for relapse warning signs. The person who actively checks for the presence of relapse warning signs is likely to trigger these warning indicators into consciousness. Once they are conscious, he can take action to intervene and interrupt the symptoms.

RELAPSE IN CHRONIC DISEASE

In order to understand what causes an alcoholic to relapse, we need to discuss the process of relapse in any chronic disease. There are similarities among all chronic diseases, and they are all subject to relapse. Diabetes, heart disease, cancer, and arthritis are chronic diseases caused by a dysfunction of the body. They may be genetically predisposed; that is, there may be hereditary factors that put one person in higher risk of developing heart disease than another person. But there are environmental factors that influence development and control of the disease.

We are going to discuss the process of relapse as it exists in any chronic disease because we believe that understanding the process will enable you to apply it more effectively to alcoholism and because we believe that the principles of relapse prevention as outlined in this book, with modification, can be effectively applied to other chronic diseases.

Relapse is a process that occurs within the patient and manifests itself in a progressive pattern of behavior that reactivates the symptoms of a disease or creates related debilitating conditions in a person that has previously experienced remission from the illness. Let's look closely at this definition of relapse.

Relapse is a process. A process is an ongoing situation that can be interrupted or changed at any time rather than a static event that is over and cannot be changed.

The process of relapse occurs within the patient. Relapse patterns are formed by attitudes, values, and behavioral responses that occur inside the patient.

Relapse manifests itself in a progressive pattern of behavior. It keeps getting worse until the process is interrupted or changed.

The relapse dynamic allows the symptoms of an illness to become reactivated or causes other debilitating symptoms. The process of uninterrupted relapse can result in the onset or recurrence of symptoms that have been arrested or can result in other related symptoms. To arrest the symptoms of a disease is to control or manage it rather than to cure it.

There are two types of disease, acute and chronic. Acute disease is disease with rapid onset and rapid progression of symptoms. The time lag between physical health and obvious debilitating symptoms is very short. As a result, the human organism has little time to adjust or adapt to those debilitating symptoms as the person loses the ability to function and is acutely aware of that loss.

Chronic disease is disease in which there is a gradual onset of progressively more severe symptoms. The time lag between physical health and obvious debilitation is a long and drawn out process. The organism becomes dysfunctional one inch at a time and has the opportunity to adapt to and compensate for the disability in order to remain functional.

It is in chronic disease that the prospect of recurring relapse is high. Due to adaptation and compensation over time, a person changes his entire lifestyle and the entire spectrum of human actions on physical, psychological, behavioral, and social levels. These changes become habitual and deeply ingrained in the personality. Even if the physical symptoms are treated, the person has become psychologically, behaviorally, and socially dependent upon the continuation of the symptoms of the disease.

Recovery is a long process. If it takes a long time to get sick, it takes a long time to get well. There is an interaction between illness and personality. There are benefits and disadvantages to illness; so there are gains and losses to recovery. When the physical aspect of disease is treated without treating other aspects, the untreated levels produce an alternate disease or induce relapse to the previous disease state.

Chronic disease forces the person to adapt to and compensate for its limitation. The person develops a relationship with his illness and learns how to incorporate it into his lifestyle.

Physical habits develop that make the disease tolerable. A person with a chronic illness gets used to the feelings and physical limits of the disease. Sleep patterns change, pain tolerance changes, and body awareness changes. These changes are all designed to allow the individual to function at the fullest possible level in spite of the illness.

Psychological habits develop that allow the person to cope with the disease. These psychological habits include changes in self-concept, changes in perception and expectations of others, and changes in overall world view. Specialized psychological habits called *denial* emerge. The goal of the denial is to allow the individual to cope with the at-times-overwhelming realities of the disease by avoiding, rationalizing, or minimizing.

Behavioral habits develop. A person with a chronic disease adjusts many routine habits and daily activities. Chronic arthritis may cause a person to favor certain joints, answer the phone with the other hand, walk shorter distances. These small changes of habit can induce severe limitations in total functioning.

Social habits develop that affect not only the person with the disease but also the concerned persons that make up his life. Family roles, rules, and rituals are altered to accommodate the illness.

Disease can also have an impact upon a person's spiritual state of well being. Disease and suffering cause some people to develop a stronger sense of faith in a higher power. The nature of chronic disease causes others to doubt the existence of God and question the meaning of life. The disease can trigger an existential crisis that results in depression and alienation.

There is an internal battle that develops as the personality begins to interact and adapt to the disease. This struggle between normal personality and the limitations of disease is intense and stress producing.

Recovery means change. The habits of long-term illness must be broken, and no habits are easily broken. The new skills of returned health must be learned or relearned. Recovery carries with it the responsibility of change.

Recovery from the symptoms of chronic disease requires total treatment, treatment not only to accommodate physical recovery, but also to promote psychological recovery (the healing of attitudes and beliefs, behavioral recovery (the changing of disease-dependent habit patterns), and social recovery (providing support as the patient and the family readjust to a lifestyle of health rather than illness).

If a person recovers physically but fails to recover psychologically, behaviorally, and socially, his illness will continue to limit him. He will never fully readjust to the unresolved memories of the illness. Physical recovery alone is only partial recovery.

Alcoholism is a chronic disease with a special tendency toward relapse. There are unique physical, psychological, behavioral, and social factors that contribute to relapse in alcoholism. Alcoholism is not a socially acceptable illness. People have negative emotions, feelings, and reactions toward an alcoholic. An alcoholic also develops negative reactions toward himself that are not present in other illness. As a result, the consequences of chronic alcoholism are far more devastating. Neither the alcoholic nor those around him believe he is ill. They view him as irresponsible, immoral, or crazy.

Because of the stigma and because of the nature of the

illness, denial and rationalization are experienced not only by the alcoholic but also by those close to him. Because of a lack of uniform comprehensive diagnostic and treatment methods, misdiagnosis is frequent and treatment often improper or incomplete.

Many alcoholics do recover, but it requires a comprehensive, ongoing recovery program. There is a common misunderstanding that someone is recovered from alcoholism who has achieved abstinence from alcohol. Nothing could be further from the truth. Alcoholism has two separate categories of symptoms. The first shows itself when the alcoholic is actively drinking. The second does not become apparent until he attempts to maintain long-term abstinence.

PROGRESSION AS A TRAINING GROUND FOR RELAPSE

The person suffering from alcoholism teaches himself that he is unable to drink. This teaching is a consistent, progressive, and long-term process. Most persons suffering from alcoholism follow the same path, the same process, the same sequence of events in learning that their drinking is not normal. They learn through a logical sequence of trial and error. The problem is that during this sequence of trial and error both direct learning and indirect learning occur. The direct learning teaches them that their drinking is not normal and interferes with their ability to live a normal life. Unfortunately, the indirect learning teaches them that long-term abstinence from alcohol is not possible. In short, the indirect learning teaches them that relapse is the end result to any attempt at sobriety.

The following seven steps in the road to sobriety briefly describe the progression of alcoholism and focus upon relapse as an integral part of the disease process. The alcoholic attempts to regulate and control drinking long before attempting permanent abstinence. Short-term abstinence and modification of drinking patterns have been entrenched in life habits. The person learns how to stop drinking for short periods of time, makes himself progressively uncomfortable during that period of abstinence, and convinces himself that a return to drinking is the only logical alternative to finding peace of mind and serenity. The seven basic steps in the road to sobriety for most alcoholics are described below.

1. Unregulated Drinking: As the alcoholic drinks in accordance with his normal preferences, he finds that he develops problems. He uses a lot of alcohol, more than he would like to. It becomes expensive and time consuming but at first causes no problems. Then he begins overdrinking and getting more intoxicated than he intended. Then he finds there is a growing urgency associated with his first drinks. Once he starts, he finds he must drink; he loses control of the ability to choose when he starts to drink. He becomes confused and sick. His life becomes disrupted.

2. Attempt To Regulate Drinking By Controlling The Quantity Of Intake: The alcoholic attempts to control by setting limits. "I won't drink that much again." He has some success but finds he can't gain permanent control through conscious limitation of quantity.

3. Attempt To Control Drinking By Changing The Type Of Alcoholic Beverage Consumed: The alcoholic changes from bourbon to scotch, from scotch to wine, from wine to beer. He tests the belief that "bourbon (or wine, or beer) isn't good for me, and with another type of alcohol I may be able to get back in charge of myself and my drinking." He hasn't yet learned that it is the alcohol and not the type of alcohol that activates the disease process that is being experienced.

4. The Attempt To Control Drinking By Pursuing Definite Periods Of Abstinence With The Goal Of Returning To Drinking: The alcoholic comes to believe that if he can stop for a month or six weeks, he'll get back in charge. And he stops for a while. He proves he can stop, but he knows he will drink again. The alcoholic can do amazing things on a short-term basis. The promise of that eventual use of alcohol is powerful. It makes the impossible easy. The proof that "I can still handle it" is worth the pain of these periods of experimental sobriety. But in the long run, things continue to get worse. The duration of these episodes of sobriety begins to diminish and the problems during these periods of sobriety become more severe.

5. The Decision To Stop Drinking Permanently Accompanied By The Refusal To Change Lifestyle: The alcoholic learns that he can't drink. He has tried everything he knows to control it and realizes that it is not possible. So he stops. What's the big deal? He stops drinking, but he keeps living in the same way. He continues to pursue a lifestyle that requires alcohol to make it complete and satisfying. He finds something is wrong, something is missing. He finds things get better for a while but then slowly become confused and frustrating. Things just don't seem to work out. He has not yet learned that alcoholism is a chronic disease that has symptoms that persist into sobriety. But he is now beginning to learn that. Recovery is not dependent upon abstinence alone. Recovery is dependent upon a change of lifestyle.

6. A Decision To Use Sedatives Or Other Mood-Altering Drugs To Assist In Controlled Drinking Or Sobriety: Here the alcoholic learns a very hard lesson. It is called cross addiction. Once addicted to alcohol, the alcoholic is predisposed to rapid addiction to barbiturates, tranquilizers, sleeping pills, etc. He does not know this and generally no one tells him.

He goes to a physician who prescribes tranquilizers in good faith, and the alcoholic takes them in good faith believing that they will help. But soon he finds that he is overdoing the pills and can't stop; he is addicted. Alcohol, pills, and marijuana do not mix without serious problems. The alcoholic can learn this either through the experiences of others or the hard way — through his own personal experiences.

7. The Decision To Stop Drinking Permanently While Pursuing A Program To Change Lifestyle: The alcoholic finally learns that the solution to alcoholism is to stop drinking, to learn about the illness, and then to change his style of living so that he can comfortably adapt to a lifestyle of total abstinence. He must learn about the chronic symptoms of alcoholism that persist into sobriety and learn how to manage these symptoms while sober.

It can be seen that this seven-step process will eventually lead the alcoholic to recognize the need for total abstinence plus a change in his alcohol-centered lifestyle. It can also be seen that the person is learning indirectly the habit of relapse. The alcoholic is learning a failure pattern that, unless interrupted through specific relapse prevention planning, will become a permanent part of his recovery/relapse cycle.

SOBRIETY-BASED SYMPTOMS OF ALCOHOLISM

When alcohol consumption stops, recovery is only beginning. A variety of symptoms begin to emerge with abstinence that are a normal part of the disease of alcoholism. Once a person acknowledges the drinking problem and discontinues the use of alcohol, the real battle for sobriety begins. Understanding of these symptoms and appropriate treatment are necessary for full recovery.

THE ACUTE ABSTINENCE SYNDROME (AAS)

Recovery begins with removing alcohol from the body. Withdrawal symptoms occur as the blood alcohol level drops below that which the alcoholic's body has come to need. The acute abstinence syndrome can manifest itself in two types. Type 1 is marked by central nervous system agitation and manifests itself in tremor, hallucinosis, delirium, and convulsive seizure. Type 2 is marked by internal anguish and manifests itself in a progressive feeling of internal agitation (the feeling of being torn apart inside), an increase in the symptoms of physical stress, elevation in blood pressure and pulse and respiration, increase in agitated or threatening behavior, progressive reports of discomfort and fear of behavioral loss of control.

While experiencing either type or any stage of AAS, a patient should be observed very carefully. Both medical and behavioral management are essential. In most cases medication is appropriate to prevent the body from overreacting to the stress of being without alcohol. Behavioral management consists of individual attention, talking about the pain and anxiety, stress management exercises, and reassurance that what is happening is normal, predictable, and will come to an end.

The seriousness of AAS should never be underestimated. Anyone suffering withdrawal symptoms needs support, and if there is any question about the severity, medical care should be sought.

POST ACUTE WITHDRAWAL SYNDROME (PAW)

Alcoholism causes brain and central nervous system damage that manifests itself in post acute withdrawal symptoms that emerge gradually after the patient stabilizes from AAS. The major symptoms of post acute withdrawal are thought process impairments, emotional process impairments, short-term memory impairments, stress sensitivity, and overreaction to stress.

Counseling For Relapse Prevention

Thought process impairment manifests itself in confusion and in narrow, rigid, and repetitive thought patterns. There is difficulty in understanding abstract principles and casual relationships. The ability to concentrate is affected and thoughts are often scattered, circular, or chaotic. Memory problems result from the inability to transfer short-term memory into long-term memory resulting in the tendency to forget things within twenty minutes of the learning experience.

Emotional process impairment manifests itself in emotional overreaction or emotional numbness. There is lowered stress tolerance as well as overreaction to stress. There is a direct relationship between stress and the severity of the symptoms of PAW. Stress intensifies PAW; the severity of PAW creates stress which further intensifies PAW.

When the thoughts of the recovering alcoholic become chaotic and confused, when he finds himself unable to concentrate or to remember, when he finds himself overreacting emotionally or in response to normal stress, he may believe he is going crazy. Recovering alcoholics need education about post acute withdrawal in order to realize that the symptoms are normal during recovery.

The symptoms produced by the post acute withdrawal syndrome are reversible with abstinence, as the neurological damage begins to heal itself and as the patient learns methods to adapt and compensate through lifestyle changes to allow productive and meaningful living in spite of the presence of ongoing symptoms. Recovery from this damage requires abstinence. The damage itself interferes with the ability to abstain. This is the paradox of recovery. Alcohol has the ability to temporarily reverse the symptoms of that damage. If a person drinks, he will think clearly for a little while, be able to have normal feelings and emotions for a little while, feel healthy for a little while. Unfortunately, the disease will eventually trigger a loss of control that once again destroys these functions.

In the controlled setting of a treatment program the severity of PAW may be extremely mild. Because the condition is stress sensitive, the impairments may suddenly become severe when a person is confronted with a situation of high stress. The patient needs to learn about PAW and methods of control when stress levels are low in order to be able to manage the symptoms when they occur.

It was once believed that neurological damage was irreversible. Recent clinical experience, however, indicates that, in spite of the fact that there is real nervous system damage, much of the impairment caused by this damage is reversible.

There are two theories that account for the ability to reverse the symptoms of neurological damage. The first is the theory that brain cells actually regenerate. This theory is controversial and is challenged by many neurological experts although there are studies that indicate reduced levels of cerebral cortical atrophy after two years of sobriety.

The second theory that accounts for the ability of the alcoholic to recover in spite of damage to the nervous system is the theory of adaptation. It is commonly accepted that the average adult uses less than one-third of the brain cells he is born with. When certain areas of the cerebral cortex are damaged by a long history of drinking, there are still large numbers of brain cells that have never been challenged to perform. If during the recovery process the recovering person regularly and consistently challenges himself to perform difficult tasks, previously unused brain cells can be called into action and begin doing the job of the damaged brain areas.

The patient must make a commitment to become involved in a daily structured program of recovery that will challenge him to relearn thought patterns, emotional habits, and behavioral patterns that have been crippled in the course of the developing disease. Any person who makes a commitment to such a daily program of recovery has an excellent chance of regaining most of his functional capabilities and living a normal life.

Patients can learn to manage the symptoms of post acute withdrawal through a program of education, stress management, diet, exercise, relaxation, and life-management skills training.

Education about the effects of PAW can assist the patient in understanding the disorder. Relating it to the symptoms they are experiencing gives them hope for recovery and a model by which to understand their behavior.

There is a direct correlation between elevated stress and the severity of PAW. Each tends to intensify the other. Stress aggravates PAW and makes it more severe; the intensity of PAW creates stress which further aggravates it. Patients can be taught skills with which to identify sources of stress and skills in decision making and problem solving to facilitate reduction of stress.

Properly structured eating habits involving a well-balanced, high-protein, low-carbohydrate diet act to reduce the effects of PAW. Excessive amounts of sweets, caffeine, and nicotine should be avoided.

Relaxation exercises can be used as a tool for neurological retraining and stress reduction. Exercise helps rebuild the body while also reducing stress. Regular habits in daily living provide needed structure and stability that reduce anxiety and enhance efficient functioning and confidence.

As the neurological damage begins to heal itself through abstinence and as the patient learns methods to adapt and compensate through lifestyle change, productive and meaningful living can be attained in spite of the symptoms of PAW.

STATE DEPENDENT LEARNING

Much of what an alcoholic has learned has been while drinking. That learning is affected by state dependent learning. What anyone learns is best recalled in the same mental state in which it was learned. What a person has learned while drinking is best practiced or recalled while at the same blood alcohol level. When the person is sober, this knowledge or skill cannot be recalled or used as easily. The person who drinks regularly becomes dependent on alcohol to function and to recall those things learned while drinking. Without alcohol he is unable to perform tasks that were easily performed while drinking. As alcohol is used with more and more life activities, the alcoholic becomes unable to function without it.

Throughout recovery the alcoholic encounters

activities that he must do for the first time sober. He cannot recall exactly how to do them. It is necessary for him to develop or redevelop behavioral skills to respond to the challenges of life without alcohol.

Sober alcoholics who do not understand the limitations created by state dependent learning cannot understand why they are unable to do many things they were able to do while drinking. They feel confused and incompetent. They avoid situations in which they may be embarrassed because of their inability to perform. Stress produced by these feelings of confusion, embarrassment, and incompetence aggravate AAS in early abstinence and PAW in later recovery. They are not aware that skills learned state dependently are easily relearned with structured practice.

The application of the knowledge of state dependent learning to the alcoholism treatment process has created a major advance in the ability to treat social skill deficiencies. By identifying which social and behavioral skills were initially learned and reinforced under the influence of alcohol it becomes possible to identify behavioral impairment areas that often went unnoticed in treatment.

Initial clinical experience in treating state dependent learning disorders indicates that, once identified, state dependently learned skills can be rapidly relearned if the patient recognizes and accepts the impairment and participates in a process of structured skill relearning that involves the use of both mental rehearsal and actual role play experience.

In a controlled setting of a group or individual counseling session the situation that demands skills retraining is recreated and appropriate workup steps are developed. The skills are broken down into small components, practiced until they become habitual, and then assembled into the total action.

ADJUSTMENT REACTIONS TO ABSTINENCE

While alcoholism is a primary physiological disease, dependence can develop psychologically, behaviorally, and socially as well as physically. Physical dependence is marked by pathological use, tolerance, and withdrawal symptoms. Psychological dependence develops as the alcoholic uses alcohol to experience pleasure and to relieve pain. He is dependent on alcohol to feel good (or better).

Behavioral dependence develops as the alcoholic learns to function with the help of alcohol and feels incompetent or unable to perform appropriately without it. Because of state dependent learning, the alcoholic finds it difficult, without alcohol, to remember how to do certain tasks and is dependent on alcohol to behave appropriately.

Social dependence results from an alcohol-centered lifestyle. As the alcoholic slowly adjusts his life to assure access to alcohol, friendships and relationships change to allow and support drinking and to provide protection from the consequences of drinking behavior. All social activities are alcohol related and the alcoholic does not know how to function socially without drinking.

Once the patient develops an alcohol-centered lifestyle and an alcohol-based personality, he is totally dependent upon alcohol for effective life functioning.

Counseling For Relapse Prevention

Even though progressive loss of control creates problems for him, the use of alcohol as a positive life-management tool is still very strong. When the positive aspects of alcohol as a coping tool are removed, the patient must adjust and learn new methods of coping with physical and emotional pain, day-to-day problems, and social pressure to drink. This adjustment requires change, and all change creates stress. As a result, an adjustment reaction often develops.

An adjustment reaction is a normal emotional and behavioral response to imposed change and, in its mild or moderate form, generally responds to appropriate treatment.

When dysfunctional living becomes a habit, it will continue indefinitely unless the person takes conscious and disciplined action to reverse the habit formation. Therefore, a large component of recovery is habit change. A person must learn how to change the habits of daily living. The function of treatment is to identify the adjustment reactions to abstinence and develop a structured program to interrupt dysfunctional living patterns and replace them with more productive life habits that are conducive to long-term sobriety.

DENIAL

All denial of alcoholism is normal. In certain individuals the denial patterns are supported and reinforced by a cluster of physical, psychological, behavioral, social, and spiritual impairments. The acute abstinence syndrome or post acute withdrawal may interfere with the patient's ability to think clearly. The need to be extremely independent and self-reliant may create the belief that to admit alcoholism would be to destroy personal identity. The person may be in the habit of denying any discomfort or of viewing the world unrealistically. There may be significant people in the person's life who reinforce the mistaken belief that he is not alcoholic and can drink normally. While denial of alcoholism is normal, it must be interrupted if treatment is to be effective.

Acceptance of the disease of alcoholism does not necessarily interrupt all denial patterns. Sobriety-based denial may continue. This may take the form of denial of personal shortcomings or personal problems. The person may deny the possibility of relapse or the need for an ongoing plan to prevent relapse. There may be denial of the need for a change in lifestyle to support sobriety. A *searching and fearless moral inventory* as described in the fourth step of AA is necessary to interrupt sobriety-based denial that may be blocking the recovery process or limiting the person to partial recovery.

ALCOHOL CRAVINGS

The nature of alcohol cravings has never been fully established, but a percentage of patients do report that they experience obsession and compulsion to use alcohol. They feel compelled to drink and develop definite cravings for the effect. These cravings, if they attack a person at a vulnerable spot, can by themselves be a primary cause of relapse.

Anyone who experiences alcohol cravings should have a plan of action that can be utilized at any time cravings occur. This plan of action should involve other people and an environment in which the need for alcohol consumption will be reduced and in which drinking is not likely to occur. People who encourage drinking or places where alcohol is readily available should be avoided if alcohol cravings occur.

PERSONALITY STYLES

People respond to abstinence with a variety of attitudes and beliefs and personality styles, some of which prevent them from maintaining a successful recovery program. The personality styles fall into three self-defeating patterns. The first we call *extreme independence.* People who are extremely independent believe they must be so independent that they can't accept help from anyone. They believe that they must face life alone and that no one can or will help them. They cannot accept the reality of powerlessness that is a part of recovery from alcoholism nor the need to rely on others. They believe they can make it by themselves and set expectations for themselves that they cannot fulfill.

The second self-defeating attitude is called *extreme dependence,* the belief that one cannot function independently. Such people do not recognize any personal strengths and rely on others in order to function. They tend to attract the type of people who dominate them in exchange for the excessive support they demand. These people sabotage their own recovery by placing all the responsibility on others and refusing to take appropriate responsibility for their own recovery. The message they give to others is, "Take care of me or I will drink."

The third self-defeating personality style is *counter-dependence*. The person who is counterdependent appears to be extremely independent, but is actually deeply insecure. He acts strong and confident while in reality he feels weak and helpless. He protects the illusion of strength and competence by manipulating others into doing things for him and taking the credit. He convinces himself and others that he is doing what is necessary to recover while evading the real issues to be faced.

In order to recover, a person must develop a *functionally independent* personality. He must recognize that he can function independently but that he needs others for a balanced life. A person with a functionally independent personality has an integrated approach to life. He recognizes his strengths and abilities and is capable of acting independently; yet he acknowledges his limitations and is willing to ask for and receive help in those areas. He is willing to take responsibility for his own recovery with the appropriate help from other people and a Higher Power.

THE RECOVERY/RELAPSE PROCESS

Recovery from alcoholism is much like walking up a down escalator. There is no such thing as standing still. When the recovering person attempts to stand still he finds himself moving backwards. Both recovery and relapse are ongoing processes rather than events. Most people tend to view recovery as an event. "Once I finish treatment, I experience the event of recovery and I am cured forever." They also tend to view relapse as the event of drinking. "If I don't start using alcohol, I will automatically remain recovered."

A process is different from an event. An event is a phenomenon that has a beginning, a middle, and an end. Once an event has taken place, it is unchangeable. A process can be changed or interrupted at any time. It is ongoing. It is occurring; it is not fixed in time. To perceive a process as an event blocks change. Death is an event; grief is a process. To perceive grief as an event locks one into grief as though it were the event of death. Death is fixed in time and cannot be changed. Grief is a process that can be interrupted or changed at any time. Recovery is not an event; it is a process. Relapse is not an event; it is a process.

The first step of recovery is to stop the intake of alcohol. Immediately after an alcoholic stops drinking, there is a period of physical illness called the acute abstinence syndrome (AAS) during which time the person withdraws physically and psychologically from alcohol.

Once the alcoholic has stopped drinking and has

detoxified from the poisonous effects of alcohol, he will respond to abstinence by becoming involved in the process of recovery or the process of relapse. It is impossible to be involved in both processes at the same time. The alcoholic is either in the process of recovering, or he is in the process of relapsing.

An alcoholic gets intoxicated through neglect of responsible living patterns rather than conscious preparations. It's what he doesn't do that induces relapse. (Some persons do consciously and overtly plan a return to drinking despite known and disastrous consequences. Such overt relapse patterns require specialized and intensive treatment.)

Relapse is not an event; it is a process subject to change or interruption. Relapse patterns in the alcoholic begin long before the first drink. There are warning signs and symptoms that pave the way. These symptoms can act as early warning signals to the patient and his family. By understanding the process, the unnecessary pain of relapse can be avoided.

This leads to two questions in the patient's mind. *What are the indications that I am in the process of recovering?* and *What are the indications that I am in the process of relapsing?* With that in mind, let's look at the process of successful recovery and determine what we, as alcoholism professionals, know about recovery. Then we will look at the dynamic of relapse in order to begin to establish methods to prevent it. These in-depth models of the recovery/relapse process set the stage for the in-depth diagnosis and treatment of the relapse dynamic itself.

The Relapse/Recovery Dynamic

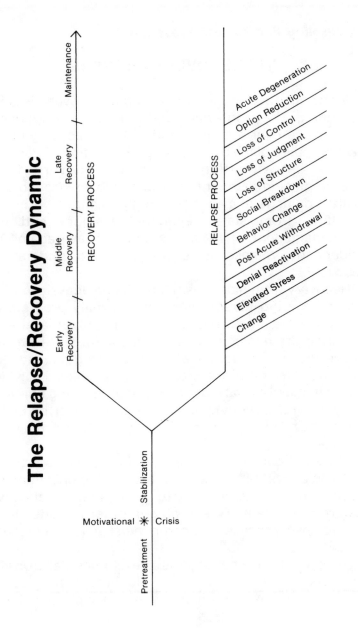

THE RECOVERY PROCESS

When alcohol consumption stops, recovery is only beginning. The progression of the disease of alcoholism takes place over a long period of time; recovery must, likewise, take place over a long period of time. Recovery means detoxification; it means recovery from neurological impairment; it means recovery from organ system damage; it means learning to manage problems resulting from state dependent memory and life mismanagement. It means learning to live again. To understand relapse it is necessary to understand recovery.

Recovery from alcoholism must be an active process. The recovering person must work a daily program of recovery. He must remind himself daily that he is suffering from alcoholism. He must further have an active recovery program which provides guidelines for effective thinking and reasoning, problem solving, regulating emotional reactions, and structuring time and daily activities. As long as he is actively involved in the productive living that is recovery, he need not fear relapse.

The alcoholic does not need to do anything special in order to activate the relapse dynamic. The only thing he needs to do is to neglect to implement an effective recovery program. This is why, in order to understand the relapse process, a person must also understand recovery.

Recovery from alcoholism is a developmental process. The person recovering from alcoholism progresses through a series of predictable recovery periods. Each recovery period is composed of specific phases. Each phase requires the completion of specific recovery tasks. These phases and tasks are developmental in nature, comparable to the stages of childhood development. As children grow, they pass through a series of developmental stages. Each stage has its specific tasks that must be accomplished in order for the children to prepare for the more advanced tasks that await them as they grow and mature.

The recovery process is very similar. The patient must grow and mature through phases of recovery. Each phase is marked by specific recovery tasks. These recovery tasks must be successfully completed in a specific order to prepare the patient to meet the challenges of advanced recovery.

Treatment incompletion is a major cause of relapse. Our current treatment technology does not adequately address the treatment needs of early or late recovery. Traditional treatment is focused primarily upon the tasks of middle recovery. As a result, we find patients dropping out of treatment in the early period because their needs are not being met. These patients generally return to drinking. We find another population of patients who maintain treatment for three to six months. They exhaust the resources of our current treatment technology, experience problems with advanced recovery, and find very few treatment resources available to them. As a result, many of these patients also return to drinking.

In order to understand this process of treatment incompletion and how it contributes to the relapse process, let's take a look at the developmental model of recovery from alcoholism.

THE DEVELOPMENTAL MODEL OF RECOVERY

The recovery process from alcoholism begins with a pretreatment period and moves through the periods of stabilization, early, middle, and late recovery. The recovering process ends when a patient enters remission. A patient is in remission when he has maintained abstinence from all alcohol and mood-altering drugs, reversed all impairments and life problems that were caused by alcoholism, and demonstrated progressive improvement in the quality of his lifestyle. Recovery is, therefore, a progressive movement through specific phases of partial recovery. Since alcoholism is a chronic and incurable disease, continuous maintenance of a recovery program is necessary even after remission is achieved. This ongoing period marks the final phase, namely the maintenance period.

PRETREATMENT. The pretreatment period unfolds before the patient ever encounters the professional helping community. The disease of alcoholism becomes a teacher. The disease slowly but surely teaches the alcoholic that he can't drink. This teaching unfolds through the law of consequence. As the disease progresses, the consequences of continued drinking become more severe until finally the person is forced to recognize that his use of alcohol is not normal. His denial breaks and he recognizes that something is seriously wrong. The process of learning by experience that controlled alcohol use is not possible is pretreatment. The end result of the pretreatment process is often called *hitting bottom.*

It was once believed that there was nothing that could be done to help a patient recover until he hit bottom. Recent research, however, indicates that there are a variety of approaches to pretreatment that can positively motivate a person to pursue initial treatment. Motivated by initial treatment, many achieve long-term recovery. These techniques are part of what is called intervention technology. The primary vehicles for intervention are the job (occupational intervention), the family (family intervention), the medical treatment community (medical intervention), and the crisis management network (crisis management).

There is generally an event called the *motivational crisis* that marks the transition between the pretreatment period and the stabilization period of recovery. The motivational crisis is an event that results in the alcoholic recognizing that something is seriously wrong, that there has been a pattern of progressive problems, and that he needs help in understanding and solving those problems. The motivational crisis is often triggered because significant others in the person's life recognize the destructive nature of this disease progression and stop enabling the process to continue. They begin actively encouraging the alcoholic to seek treatment.

STABILIZATION. The stabilization period of recovery includes acute stabilization (detoxification), and a period of motivational counseling. The major tasks of this period are stabilizing the patient physically and psychologically so that he can recognize the emerging pattern of crisis, relate that pattern of crisis to drinking, enter a period of initial abstinence, undergo an initial diagnostic presentation, and develop the motivation to pursue long-term treatment. Stabilization includes the development of an initial professionally regulated sobriety plan. The patient does not have sufficient knowledge or motivation at this point to develop a self-regulated sobriety plan but needs the direction offered by a professionally developed plan.

During the stabilization phase, the patient is physically and psychologically unstable. He is very sick. As a result, much of the cognitive therapy and motivational counseling will not be retained. As the patient stabilizes neurologically and psychologically, his previous defenses will return. Therefore, the treatment tasks of the stabilization phase must be repeated and reinforced in early recovery after the patient has achieved significant physical, neurological, and psychological stabilization.

EARLY RECOVERY. The early treatment period completes the task of emotionally and cognitively processing the motivational crisis and acute stabilization period. An intensive and in-depth diagnostic presentation must be completed again and must focus on both alcoholism and alcohol-related life problems that will persist into recovery. If a family or employer confrontation occurred in the stabilization period, it should be repeated in the early recovery period. This early recovery period is vital to the patient in establishing a strong belief that he is an alcoholic and a strong motivation to recover through a structured program of lifestyle change.

MIDDLE RECOVERY. The middle period of recovery occurs after the patient has made a commitment to long-term treatment. The first task of middle recovery is to overcome the demoralization which commonly emerges once the patient makes the decision to recover. The decision to recover is based on the powerful impact of the diagnostic presentation. It shatters the patient's perception of himself, his life, and his alcohol use. This initial demoralization is used to motivate the patient into treatment. The patient knows something is seriously wrong and the diagnostic presentation builds an overwhelming and undeniable argument that alcoholism is its cause.

The motivational period convinces the patient that recovery is possible if treatment is pursued. In middle recovery the excitement is over. Things quiet down. The patient must face himself honestly and deal with the questions: Have I done the right thing? Am I really an alcoholic? Am I really responsible for this? Do I really need this intensity of treatment? Can I live without alcohol? Can I rebuild my life?

Once this demoralization period is resolved, the patient must learn about his illness, struggle with full emotional acceptance of the disease and the demands of the recovery program. Acceptance is achieved when the internal dissonance, the conflict between the mind and the emotions, is resolved. A person accepts the diagnosis of alcoholism when he recognizes that recovery is worth the price. The final step of the middle recovery period is building a structured self-regulated sobriety plan. By this time the patient should be sufficiently informed and motivated to make decisions about his own recovery and to develop a plan to carry them out.

Current treatment methods are primarily designed to assist patients in meeting the developmental tasks of middle recovery. The tasks of early recovery are generally skipped over lightly. It is assumed that the tasks of early recovery were successfully completed in the pretreatment and stabilization periods. Unfortunately, for many patients this is not the case. They have entered the treatment process without completing the basic recovery tasks of stabilization and early treatment. As a result they are not prepared to successfully complete the tasks of middle recovery. These patients often struggle with treatment methods that are designed to cope with the tasks of middle recovery, but no matter how hard they try, they fail. They fail because they have not been prepared for this phase of recovery.

Instead of recognizing the limitations of the treatment technology, the professional often blames the patient for the failure and often responds with hard confrontation. In spite of the best intentions they are actually punishing patients for the inability to respond to treatment. The only problem with hard confrontation is that, in spite of popular belief, it is not effective in the treatment of alcoholism. Hard confrontation generally accomplishes one of two things. Either the defenses of the patient are reinforced and he becomes more resistant to treatment, or he merely complies with the external requirements of treatment without undergoing any real change of perception or motivation.

LATE RECOVERY. The late period of recovery deals with the need to stabilize alcohol-related life problems and to identify and resolve other life problems that may be unrelated to alcoholism. Once these problems are resolved, the patient must explore his current value systems and learn how to distinguish alcohol-centered values from sobriety-centered values. He must also identify the self-defeating personality styles that are highly correlated with relapse and begin a long-term program of personality change. The new personality styles must lead to an integrated and balanced way of life. During this period, the patient reexamines his personal life history and family history. He generally undertakes to establish or reestablish a sense of spiritual identity. As the person approaches full remission, the focus of his attention is drawn more and more strongly to life and living. He learns to live again in a manner that is highly compatible with sobriety and generates, as a consequence, a sense of serenity and peace of mind.

MAINTENANCE. Alcoholism is a chronic disease, and the disease itself has little to do with alcohol. The essence of the disease is the compulsion within the individual that creates a tendency towards alcohol-centered thinking, alcohol-centered living, and the desire to use alcohol in spite of known destructive consequences. Alcoholism is also the long-term neurological, personality, and lifestyle damage that follows a patient into recovery. The ghosts of this disease haunt the recovering patient for life. Full remission can only be maintained by recognizing the life-long need for a strong maintenance plan consisting of a daily program of ongoing recovery and personal growth.

Unfortunately, current treatment methods and delivery systems are geared towards meeting the needs of the patient in his first three to six months of recovery. It is somehow assumed that if a person can make it through that critical first six months, he can make it on his own with the help of Alcoholics Anonymous. For some this is true, but for others, the relapse-prone patients, nothing could be further from the truth. The needs of advanced recovery are very different from those of early recovery. But the failure to meet those needs is the same — relapse. — relapse.

If relapse prevention is to become a reality, a method must be designed to provide structured treatment that is appropriate to the needs of the recovering person over the entire recovery period, which means two to three years. Alcoholism is a life-long disease. It requires life-long treatment. As a result of our lack of treatment resources designed to meet the needs of early and late recovery, many patients relapse in spite of their honest efforts at maintaining sobriety. In spite of their best efforts to help their patients, many treatment professionals fail, not because they are incompetent, but simply because they are unaware of the long-term developmental process of recovery.

THE RELAPSE PROCESS

Recovery from alcoholism is often complicated by a variety of factors. In the long run, it is the patient's response to the problems and complications that determine whether he will maintain long-term remission or enter a relapse dynamic and eventually return to drinking.

Studies of the relapse process have demonstrated that there are objective and predictable warning signs of relapse that are present long before the patient starts drinking. The patient doesn't need to do anything special in order to make these symptoms appear. All he needs to do is to fail to take appropriate steps in his recovery program and these relapse warning symptoms will spontaneously develop. When the warning signs emerge, the patient is usually unaware of their presence. Relapse is not a conscious choice, but the end result of an unconscious, but progressive, sequence of warning signs.

These warning signs begin with very mild indicators of change in thought patterns, emotional process, and behavior. The symptoms are progressive. They will continue to become more and more severe unless the patient becomes aware of their presence and takes definite action to interrupt the symptom progression.

The end result of this progression of warning signs is that the patient begins unconsciously removing behavioral alternatives. His range of problem-solving options continues to shrink until he believes that his only possible alternatives are insanity, suicide, physical or emotional collapse, or drinking. Most patients choose to return to drinking in order to avoid a nervous breakdown or suicide. Many patients, however, remain sober and find themselves in progressive difficulties that lead to suicide attempts, severe emotional breakdowns, physical collapse, development of a major stress-related illness, or accident proneness.

The relapse dynamic is reversible if the patient receives appropriate treatment. Initial clinical work with relapse prevention planning indicates that the major component of relapse prevention is teaching patients about the warning signs of relapse and involving them in a regular process of personal inventory to determine if any warning signs have developed in their lives. With conscious awareness of the warning signs, it is possible to take action to reverse the effects and thus interrupt the relapse dynamic.

It is helpful for the counselor to understand in detail the process of the relapse dynamic. A complete description of the 37 typical warning signs that precede relapse is reviewed below. It is also important that the counselor and patient understand the dynamics by which this progression operates. To shed more light upon the dynamics of relapse, the warning signs have been summarized in a progressive 11-step summary model.

These two models, the 37 warning signs of relapse and the relapse summary model, become useful tools in the relapse prevention planning process. Their exact use will be reviewed in the section on relapse prevention planning.

WARNING SIGNS OF RELAPSE

A uniform pattern of relapse has been identified. Relapse does not begin with the first drink. Relapse begins in a behavioral dynamic which reactivates patterns of denial, isolation, elevated stress, and impaired judgment. The pattern of this behavior set-up was identified in 1973 by the author through the completion of clinical interviews with 118 alcoholic patients who met the following criteria: They had completed a 21- or 28-day rehabilitation treatment program. They had been discharged with the conscious intention of remaining permanently sober. They had eventually returned to loss-of-control consumption in spite of initial commitments to remain sober. The results of this clinical research were compiled in the form of a relapse chart depicting the symptoms leading to a relapse. The most commonly reported symptoms follow.

1. *Apprehension About Well-Being:* Alcoholics reported an initial sense of fear and uncertainty. There was a lack of confidence in the ability to stay sober. This apprehension was often extremely short-lived.

2. *Denial:* Patients reactivated denial systems in order to cope with apprehension and resultant anxiety and stress. The denial systems reactivated in this stage of the relapse dynamic tend to correspond with the denial systems utilized to deny the presence of alcoholism during the initial phase of treatment. Most patients were aware of this denial with hindsight but reported that they were unaware of this denial process while experiencing it.

3. *Adamant Commitment To Sobriety:* The patients convinced themselves they would *never drink again.* This self-persuasion was sometimes overt and blatant but most often constituted a very private decision. Many patients reported fear or apprehension of sharing that conviction with their therapists or with members of AA. Once patients convinced themselves they would never drink again, the urgency of pursuing a daily program of recovery diminished.

4. *Compulsive Attempts To Impose Sobriety On*

Others: This attempt to impose sobriety or individual standards for recovery on others was seldom overt. It was generally private judgments about the drinking of friends and spouses and the quality of the sobriety programs of fellow recovering alcoholics. When dealing with the issues of sobriety, the patients began to focus more on what others were doing than on what they were doing.

5. *Defensiveness:* Patients reported a noticeable increase in their defensiveness when talking about their problems or recovery programs.

6. *Compulsive Behavior:* Behavior patterns became rigid and repetitive. The alcoholics tended to control conversational involvement either through monopoly or silence. The tendency towards overwork and compulsive involvement in activities began to appear. Nonstructured involvement with people was avoided.

7. *Impulsive Behavior:* Patterns of compulsive behaviors began to be interrupted by impulsive reactions. In many cases the impulse was overreaction to acute episodes of stress. There were also reports of impulsive activities being the culmination of a chronic stress situation. Many times these overreactions to stress formed the basis of decisions which affected major life areas and commitments to ongoing treatment.

8. *Tendencies Toward Loneliness:* Patterns of isolation and avoidance increased. There were generally valid reasons and excuses for this isolation. Patients reported short episodes of intense loneliness at increasing intervals. These episodes were generally dealt with by reactivating compulsive or impulsive behavior patterns rather than by pursuing responsible involvement with other people.

9. Tunnel Vision: Patients tended to view their lives in isolated fragments. They would focus exclusively on one area, preoccupy themselves with it, and avoid looking at other areas. Sometimes preoccupation was with the positive aspects thus creating a delusion of security and well-being. Others preoccupied themselves with the negative aspects thus assuming victim positions which confirmed the belief that they were helpless and being treated unfairly.

10. Minor Depression: Symptoms of depression began to appear and persist. Listlessness, flat affect, oversleeping became common.

11. Loss Of Constructive Planning: Patients' skills at life planning began to diminish. Attention to detail subsided. Wishful thinking began to replace realistic planning.

12. Plans Begin To Fail: Due to lack of planning, failure to follow through, lack of attention to detail, or the pursuit of unrealistic objectives, plans began to fail.

13. Idle Daydreaming And Wishful Thinking: The ability to concentrate diminished and concentration was replaced with fantasy. The *If Only* syndrome became more common in conversation. The fantasies were generally of escape or of "being rescued from it all" by some unlikely set of circumstances.

14. *Feeling That Nothing Can Be Solved:* A failure pattern in sobriety was developed. In some cases the failure was real in terms of objective realities; in other cases it was imagined and based upon intangibles. The generalized perception of "I've tried my best and it isn't working out" began to develop.

15. *Immature Wish To Be Happy:* Conversational content and thought patterns become vague and generalized. The desire to "be happy" or "have things work out" became more common without ever defining what was necessary to be happy or have things work out.

16. *Periods Of Confusion:* The episodes of confusion increased in terms of frequency, duration, and severity of behavioral impairment.

17. *Irritation With Friends:* Social involvement including friends and intimate relationships, as well as treatment relationships formed with therapists and AA members, became strained and conflictual. The conflictual nature increased as confrontation of the alcoholic's progressively degenerating behavior increased.

18. *Easily Angered:* Episodes of anger, frustration, resentment, and irritability increased. Overreaction became more frequent. Often the fear of extreme overreaction, to the point of violence, seriously increased the level of stress and anxiety.

19. *Irregular Eating Habits:* Patients began over-eating or undereating. The regular structure of meals was disrupted. Well-balanced meals were often replaced by less nourishing junk foods.

20. *Listlessness:* Extended periods of inability to initiate action developed. These were marked by inability to concentrate, anxiety and severe feelings of apprehension. Patients often reported this as a feeling of being trapped or of having no way out.

21. *Irregular Sleeping Habits:* Episodes of insomnia were reported. Nights of restlessness and fitful sleep were reported. Episodes of sleeping marathons of 12 to 20 hours were reported at intervals varying between 6 and 15 days. These sleeping marathons apparently resulted from exhaustion.

22. *Progressive Loss Of Daily Structure:* Daily routines became haphazard. Regular hours of retiring and rising disappeared. Inability to sleep resulted in oversleeping. Meal structures disappeared. Complaints of inability to keep appointments became more common and social planning decreased. Patients reported feeling rushed and overburdened at times and then faced large blocks of idle time in which they didn't know what to do. An inability to follow through on plans and decisions was also reported. The patients reported they knew what they should do but were unable to overcome strong feelings of tension, frustration, fear, or anxiety that prevented them from following through.

23. *Periods Of Deep Depression:* Depression became more severe, more frequent, more disruptive, and longer in duration. These periods generally occurred during nonstructured time periods and were amplified by fatigue and hunger. During these periods the patient tended toward isolation and reacted to human contact with irritability and anger while, at the same time, complaining that nobody cared.

24. *Irregular Attendance At Treatment Meetings:* Attendance at AA became sporadic. Therapy appointments were scheduled and then missed. Attendance at treatment groups and home AA meetings became sporadic. Rationalization patterns developed to justify this. The effectiveness of AA and treatment was discounted. Treatment lost a priority ranking in the patient value system.

25. *Development Of An "I Don't Care" Attitude:* Patients generally reported this *I don't care* stance masked a feeling of helplessness and extremely poor self-image.

26. *Open Rejection Of Help:* Patients cut themselves off from viable sources of help. This was sometimes accomplished dramatically through fits of anger or open discounts. Other times it was done through quiet withdrawal.

27. *Dissatisfaction With Life:* Patients began to think "things are so bad now I might as well get drunk because they can't get worse." Rationalizations, tunnel vision, and wishful thinking began to give way to the harsh reality of how totally unmanageable life had become in the course of this period of abstinence.

28. Feelings Of Powerlessness And Helplessness: This was marked by an inability to initiate action. Thought processes were scattered, judgment was distorted, concentration and abstract thinking abilities were impaired. were impaired.

29. Self-Pity: Patients became indulgent in self-pity. This is often called the PLOM (Poor Little Old Me) Syndrome. This self-pity often was used as an attention-getting device at AA and with family members.

30. Thoughts Of Social Drinking: The patients realized that drinking could normalize many of the feelings and emotions they were experiencing. The hope that perhaps they could again drink in a controlled fashion began to emerge. Sometimes the thought was challenged and put out of conscious thought; other times it was entertained. Again, with hindsight, the patients realized they had few other alternatives but drinking. They felt they were facing a choice between insanity, suicide, or a return to drinking.

31. Conscious Lying: Denial and rationalization became such extreme processes that even the alcoholics began to recognize the lies and deceptions. In spite of this recognition, they felt unable to interrupt the pattern.

32. *Complete Loss Of Self-Confidence:* The patients felt they could not get out of this trap no matter how hard they tried. They became overwhelmed by the inability to think clearly or initiate action.

33. *Unreasonable Resentments:* The patients felt severe anger with the world in general and the inability to function. This anger was sometimes generalized; at other times focused at particular scapegoats; at other times turned against themselves.

34. *Discontinuing All Treatment:* Attendance at AA stopped completely. Patients who were taking Antabuse reported episodes of forgetting to take it or manipulating to avoid taking it regularly. When a helping person relationship was part of the treatment, strain and eventual termination of that relationship resulted. Patients dropped out of professional treatment in spite of a realization that they were acting irrationally and needed help.

35. *Overwhelming Loneliness, Frustration, Anger, And Tension:* The patient reported feeling totally overwhelmed and feeling there was no available option except returning to drinking, suicide, or insanity. The fear of insanity was intense. There were also intense feelings of helplessness and desperation. Often drinking was an impulsive behavior with little or no conscious preplanning.

36. *Start Of Controlled Drinking:* The efforts at control took two general patterns: the effort to control quantities while drinking on a regular basis and the effort to engage in one short-term and low-consequential binge.

37. *Loss Of Control:* The ability to control was lost, sometimes very quickly, sometimes after varying patterns of controlled drinking. The patient, however, quickly returned to alcoholic drinking which was marked by symptoms as severe or more severe than presented during the last episode of active alcoholism.

The discovery that there are predictable symptoms or warning signs that precede a return to alcohol use in the alcoholic has created some new and challenging questions and has pointed to a radical new approach to the treatment of the alcoholic who has a history of relapse.

The primary questions raised by the discovery of relapse warning signs has been: What causes these predictable warning signs to develop? Is it possible that there are underlying neurological or psychological problems that are being reflected in these behavioral warning signs? Do different types of patients experience different patterns of warning signs?

The radical new approach to treatment suggested by the presence of these warning signs is simple and straightforward: educate the patient about the presence of the warning signs, teach the patient and significant others to be alert for the relapse warning signs, and develop a treatment plan that will intervene at the first indication of relapse warning signs. The presence of relapse warning signs makes it possible to intervene before the patient returns to drinking.

SUMMARY MODEL OF THE RELAPSE DYNAMIC

The 37 warning signs can be summarized in eleven steps that carry a patient gradually from recovery toward drinking. This summary model integrates the 37 warning signs with research into the neurological and neuropsychological aspects of alcoholism. It recognizes a progression that includes the physical, psychological, behavioral, and social aspects of relapse and their relationship in the progression. By recognizing these stages in the relapse process it is possible to interrupt the progression.

1. Change: Change is a normal part of life but a major cause of stress. Change can easily trigger a response that takes a person out of the recovery process into the relapse dynamic if the person is unaware of what is happening or unprepared to manage it.

There is a common sequence of change that often initiates the relapse dynamic. It starts with a change in attitude, particularly about the need for a recovery program, and leads from there into a change of behavior and a change in life structure that interferes with the maintenance of the ongoing recovery program.

The initial change can also be an external event that

forces a patient to alter his daily structure and thus increases stress and triggers an internal change of attitude.

2. Elevated Stress: Change produces stress to which alcoholics are apt to overreact and for which they may have low tolerance.

3. Denial Reactivation: As stress levels are elevated and become critical, there is a normal tendency to deny the presence of the excessive stress and to reinitiate the denial mechanisms that accompany the disease. When the alcoholic begins using denial patterns to deal with stress similar to the denial used to deal with the acceptance of alcoholism, other associated thought processes are triggered.

4. Post Acute Withdrawal (PAW): Elevated stress intensifies the symptoms of PAW. As these symptoms — thought process, emotional process, and memory problems — intensify, stress levels are elevated even further (which increases the severity of PAW).

5. Behavior Change: As a result of the developing symptoms of PAW, reactivation of denial, and chronic elevated stress, the patient begins to act differently. He still goes to the same places and engages in the same activities, but his behavior invites unnecessary stress and sets the stage for future crisis.

6. Social Breakdown: With a change in behavior, there is a change in relationships. The alcoholic begins to interact in a different way and there is a breakdown in social structure.

7. *Loss Of Structure:* Life structure begins to break down. Recovery plans are abandoned, routine and daily habits are altered.

8. *Loss Of Judgment:* Lack of structure, lack of support systems, and increasingly severe PAW lead to confusion, disorder, and the inability to solve problems or make decisions. The alcoholic may be emotionally numb or be overreacting emotionally.

9. *Loss Of Control:* The next step is loss of control of thought processes and of behavior. The person does not make rational choices and is unable to interrupt or modify his actions.

10. *Option Reduction:* He comes to believe that he is no longer in control of his life and believes that the only alternatives available to him are insanity, physical or emotional collapse, suicide, or drinking.

11. *Acute Degeneration:* He returns to drinking or drug use; he may develop stress-related illnesses, psychiatric problems, emotional collapse, or physical exhaustion; or he may attempt suicide or become accident prone.

PARTIAL RECOVERY

Many persons suffering from alcoholism begin

recovery but fail to complete the entire process. The dynamics of partial recovery become a circular and repetitive behavior pattern, more deeply entrenched with each repetition. What happens is that the person progresses to a certain point, but unable to progress beyond that point, switches into a relapse dynamic. He moves through the process of relapse, believing himself to be in the process of recovery, until something, or some things, so severe happen that he becomes aware that he is in danger of relapse. At that point he takes some action to put himself back into a recovery process. However, his participation in the relapse process has taken its toll. He must retrace his steps and begin the recovery process in the first stage of motivational crisis.

Remember that the relapse process begins long before the first drink. Once a person begins actively participating in a relapse dynamic, he is progressively undoing the progress of treatment. What interrupts the relapse dynamic is a motivational crisis. This motivational crisis must be recognized and accepted and the person must begin working through the recovery phases again.

This process, however, is not identical to starting over. If a person interrupts the relapse dynamic early enough, he finds that his progress in successfully completing the tasks of recovery are extremely rapid and much easier than if he let the relapse dynamic unfold to its logical conclusion, namely drinking and the crisis that accompanies that.

Every time a person completes a phase in the recovery process, he begins developing the habit of successfully completing that phase. Therefore, a failure after a period of long-term sobriety does not mean the person starts over again. He already has the skill and the knowledge that he can successfully survive and complete the necessary phases of recovery. Therefore, the recovery process is easier and faster.

The patient can, however, get locked into a pattern of partial recovery. This pattern of partial recovery means he begins the recovery process and moves along to the point that he becomes frightened by the results of his self-examination. This fear of facing himself triggers the reactivation of the relapse cycle. The relapse cycle unfolds until he recognizes that he is on his way to a return to drinking. The fear of returning to drinking triggers him back into a recovery process and he begins working through the recovery phases again. Once again he reaches the point at which self-examination becomes extremely frightening. Again, he chooses not to follow through all phases of recovery and once again clicks into a relapse cycle. This pattern can repeat itself indefinitely.

Let's review this dynamic of partial recovery in more detail by conceptualizing it as a series of steps.

Step 1: The person stops drinking and stabilizes through the acute abstinence syndrome.

Step 2: The patient progresses through the initial phases of the recovery process.

Step 3: The person reaches a phase in the recovery process that he finds particularly frightening or difficult.

Step 4: The patient develops a normal sense of fear or

inadequacy in confronting the difficult challenges of the particular phase of recovery.

Step 5:   The person interprets this fear and feeling of insecurity and inadequacy as abnormal, destructive, or insurmountable.

Step 6:   The inability to deal with the fear of completing the tasks of recovery activates the relapse dynamic.

Step 7:   The person undergoes the changes in attitude that accompany the early stages of the relapse dynamic.

Step 8:   The person experiences the progressive stages in the development of the relapse dynamic.

Step 9:   The person recognizes the progressive loss of behavioral control that inevitably precedes a relapse.

Step 10:   The fear of the relapse triggers a reactivation of the recovery process and the person begins actively pursuing a positive program of recovery.

Step 11:   The patient restabilizes and progresses in recovery until he is again ready to confront the particular phase of recovery which produced a feeling of fear and insecurity before. These same feelings develop again.

Step 12:   The prospect of completing this particular phase of recovery again triggers a fear which activates the relapse dynamic.

Counseling For Relapse Prevention

Step 13: The cycle continues until such a high level of stress is generated that a complete relapse occurs or the person experiences an emotional collapse or a serious stress-related illness.

Many alcoholics experience only partial recovery. They go only so far in their recovery process but never become totally free of the self-defeating attitudes and habit patterns that accompany their alcoholism. They are enslaved by their illness in spite of the fact that they are abstinent. Their lives are better than if they were actively drinking because they are avoiding the direct and self-defeating consequences of alcohol use. But they are not free to live normal and productive lives because they are crippled by self-imposed limits of their illness. The patient suffering from partial recovery is in very high risk of relapse.

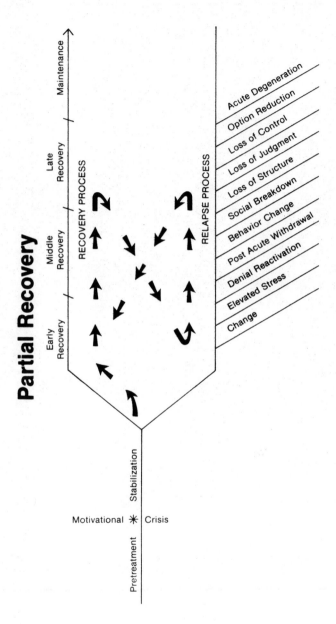

Partial Recovery

FACTORS THAT COMPLICATE RECOVERY

The developmental model of recovery describes recovery from the normal sobriety-based symptoms of alcoholism. There are, however, conditions and situations that complicate this normal recovery process. Persons experiencing these recovery complications need specialized treatment that is appropriate for their situation.

It is necessary to distinguish between the normal sobriety-based symptoms and special complicating factors in order to provide appropriate treatment. What are complicating factors and how do you recognize them? Any situation, event, or condition that interferes with the patient's ability to respond to treatment or the normal recovery process requires a special treatment plan to deal with the specific problem, stabilize the patient from the problem, and enable him to return to and respond to a regular treatment plan. Any time a patient is not responding to treatment, an evaluation should be made to identify factors that may be interfering with the ability to recover and to respond appropriately to treatment. We will discuss some of the more frequent recovery complications.

SEVERE SOBRIETY-BASED SYMPTOMS

A person who develops severe dependence upon and may present unique problems and unique treatment complications that are not present when the symptoms are less severe. When the symptoms of the acute abstinence syndrome, post acute withdrawal, state dependent learning, adjustment disorders of abstinence, denial, or alcohol craving are very severe, they interfere with the patient's ability to recognize that he is alcoholic, to enter treatment, to maintain long-term treatment, or to improve by using available treatment methods.

In its severe form, AAS is the primary cause of discharge against medical advice from acute stabilization units. Special medical and behavioral care that is specific to the needs of the patient can decrease the number of patients leaving treatment against medical advice and increase the number of patients that accept ongoing treatment for alcoholism.

The symptoms of post acute withdrawal are usually manageable with reasonable care of diet, exercise, stress management, and highly structured daily activities. From time to time the symptoms may be so debilitating that the patient is incapable of maintaining the necessary self-care program that will enable neurological healing.

The symptoms of PAW usually peak over the first 90 days of abstinence and begin to subside as a result of neurological healing over a period of six months to two years. Patients with advanced alcoholism may develop residual damage that is present for the rest of their lives.

Patients with debilitating or residual symptoms require special, intensive, and carefully monitored programs of care to reduce the severity of the syndrome and allow them to participate in other forms of treatment. The patient must be prepared to seriously invest time and effort, and must realize that ongoing recovery requires daily maintenance. Biofeedback and neurological retraining offer significant hope for more effective management of this form of the PAW syndrome.

When drinking has been a regular part of all life activities for a very long time, all life skills may be affected by state dependent learning, leaving a sober alcoholic unable to function. Fear of failure in such cases can block relearning and result in isolation and a self-defeating lifestyle. When life-management skills are severely impaired or when fear of failure or denial of impairments resulting from state dependent learning blocks relearning, a concentrated program is necessary to assess the areas of impairment, remove denial, and overcome the fears associated with attempting activities that have never been experienced sober.

When an adjustment reaction to abstinence is severe it becomes an *adjustment disorder* of abstinence. An adjustment disorder of abstinence exists when physical, psychological, behavioral, or social dependence on alcohol is so severe that the alcoholic is unable to function in that area or unable to complete certain tasks without drinking no matter how much effort is exerted. By observing adjustments to an alcohol-free life, adjustment disorders can be identified that create or maintain functional impairments and interfere with the ability to participate in or respond to treatment. These impairments require a program of retraining to overcome the specific dysfunction.

When denial is a typical and normal part of the disease process it subsides as the patient becomes actively involved in treatment and a structured recovery program. Severe and rigid denial that does not respond to traditional treatment methods is not normal. Any time severe and rigid denial patterns are present the possibility of other severe complicating factors should be considered. Unless special efforts to diagnose and treat the complications that are creating and maintaining the rigid denial are initiated, the denial pattern will block the ability to maintain sobriety and increase the risk of relapse.

Severe alcohol cravings can distract a person from treatment and create high stress that activates PAW and makes the patient vulnerable to an impulse drink or social pressure to drink. Patients who report strong alcohol cravings or a history of strong cravings should be given extra assistance and support in recovery.

Strong cravings may be triggered by accidental alcohol or drug ingestion. At times a patient may accidentally use a medication with an alcohol-based solvent or a medication that incorporates a sedative or a narcotic. Such accidental ingestion triggers a strong physical and/or psychological craving. Any time an alcoholic uses alcohol it disrupts the recovery process. Every alcoholic should be educated to observe ingredients in everything consumed and to seek assistance and support should accidental ingestion occur.

COMPLICATIONS ASSOCIATED WITH SEVERE POLYDRUG DEPENDENCE

The use of other mood-altering drugs in conjunction with alcoholism can distort the specific symptoms of alcoholism. The biochemical actions of alcohol with other drugs create unique addiction reactions and unique AAS and PAW. Usual reactions are changed or intensified when drugs and alcohol are used in combination and can create complex withdrawal symptoms. Cross addictions or multiple addictions complicate the recovery process.

The polydrug dependent person may experience difficulty in responding to traditional alcoholism treatment, especially if alcohol is not the primary drug of choice (just as a polydrug user who is primarily an alcoholic may have problems responding to traditional treatment for drug dependence). There are factors associated with the subcultures of both alcoholism and drug dependence that can be complicating variables in treatment and in the recovery process.

The recovery process is further complicated if the polydrug user has been using illegal drugs. There may be criminal proceedings, incarceration, or legal problems that are not encountered by the alcoholic or the person addicted to prescription drugs. In addition, special measures may be required to overcome or break away from a lifestyle that may have developed around illegal activity.

Research is needed into the patterns of recovery and factors that complicate recovery from polydrug dependence in order to provide more specific guidelines for the cross-addicted alcoholic.

FACTORS ASSOCIATED WITH COEXISTING PHYSICAL AND PSYCHOLOGICAL ILLNESS

Alcoholism often coexists with a variety of other physical and psychological illnesses or disorders. Alcoholism is not secondary to other physical or psychological disorders. The progression of alcoholism does, however, often create the tendency to develop coexisting problems. The discussion of these complications will be handled in two separate areas. The first area deals with typical complications related to physical illness. The second area will deal with typical complications related to psychological or psychiatric illness.

COMPLICATIONS RELATED TO PHYSICAL ILLNESS

Any acute illness can be a disruptive factor in a recovering person's life. Acute illnesses produce high levels of stress that can reactivate post acute withdrawal. Any acute episode related to a chronic illness such as cancer, heart disease, or diabetes creates stress. The person lives with fear and apprehension about his well-being.

The more severe the illness, the more restricted the patient will be in his ability to participate in any activities including treatment activities for alcoholism. This challenges the creativity and flexibility of the alcoholism counselor. He must design a recovery program that can be implemented in conjunction with the treatment and rehabilitation needs of the coexisting illness. The person must be allowed an opportunity to identify and deal with the stress-related and anxiety-related factors that are caused by the presence of the coexisting physical illness.

A major problem that complicates recovery from alcoholism is the presence of conditions that result in chronic pain. Arthritis, lower back pain, orthopedic injuries, migraine headaches are common conditions that cause long-term chronic pain that can be very debilitating, can reactivate the symptoms of post acute withdrawal, and can lead ultimately to a collapse from stress degeneration.

The counselor should recognize the presence of a coexisting pain disorder, be able to counsel about medication-free methods of pain reduction, and know of resources in the community, such as pain clinics, where the patient can be sent to receive specialized treatment in conjunction with his alcoholism treatment.

There are some physical illnesses that require the use of mood-altering medications in the course of their treatment. It is true that mood-altering chemicals are often misused or abused in medical treatment. There are conditions, however, in which the use of these medications is necessary to save a person's life or to prevent progression of the condition into a chronic or debilitating state.

This should not be construed as a recommendation that people use mood-altering drugs to deal with physical pain and physical complaints. The use of these medications should be a last alternative.

The use of the mood-altering substances will destabilize the patient's thought processes, emotional processes, and memory. He must establish a strong and specialized support structure to assure that he does not become addicted or dependent upon the chemicals and to assure that he can effectively manage his life during the period of aggravated PAW.

The physician should be fully informed of the addiction or abuse potential of the patient. The medications used should be selected to minimize the risk of abuse or addiction. The medications should be monitored in their distribution on a daily basis and no access should be afforded to ongoing open-ended prescriptions. The course of drug therapy should be as short as possible to bring about the desired corrective actions.

An example of an incident that requires the use of medications is major surgery. Major surgery requires the use of pre-operative sedatives, anesthesia, and post-operative pain medications. If the patient is appropriately prepared for the surgical procedures, however, the use of medications can be minimized and the patient can be prepared to face complications effectively without jeopardizing his long-term recovery.

For patients who experience chronic pain conditions, there are drug-free methods that can be employed to cope with the pain that can bring about a reduction in its severity. The long-term use of pain killers or other mood-altering drugs in an effort to deal with pain is counterproductive and can lead to dependence or addiction even in nonalcoholic individuals. This risk of addiction and dependence is greater in the alcoholic.

It must be recognized, however, that if we remove the option of pain killers and other mood-altering medications to help a person deal with pain disorders, we must offer other techniques that give some relief from the pain. In the absence of effective behavioral technologies that will bring about relief from pain, the patient is in high risk of relapse.

COMPLICATIONS RELATED TO PSYCHOLOGICAL OR PSYCHIATRIC DISORDERS

Although alcoholism is not caused by psychological or psychiatric problems, there is a significant number of patients suffering from alcoholism who have coexisting personality or psychiatric disorders. At times these disorders preceded the alcoholism; at other times the disorders developed in parallel with the alcoholism; in still others, they have developed after initial abstinence.

As with any other complication, the primary question that needs to be answered in designing treatment is, "What impact does this disorder have upon the patient's ability to maintain sobriety?" If the answer is that the patient is capable of maintaining initial sobriety in spite of the presence of the disorder, leave it alone. Do not attempt to treat it until the person has established and reinforced a secure and functional recovery program. Psycotherapy and treatment for psychiatric or personality disorders is extremely stressful and creates an exaggeration of personal and emotional pain before relief occurs. Many individuals can comfortably maintain a period of sobriety without directly confronting the issues of dysfunctional personality. If they are forced to confront these issues, their pain could increase to the point that the relapse dynamic is triggered.

We should recognize the presence of personality disorders and psychiatric conditions. But unless they directly interfere with the ability of the person to maintain sobriety, treatment for these conditions should be delayed until the later stages of recovery when there is a secure and established track record of sobriety.

Counseling For Relapse Prevention

Before treatment it is impossible to accurately determine if a person has personality or psychiatric disorders. The person who is drinking exhibits a number of unusual personality characteristics that could be diagnosed as any one of a variety of psychiatric disorders. These are directly caused by the toxic effects of alcohol upon the person's central nervous system. They are the result of the neurological disruption caused by the use of or withdrawal from alcohol. It is, therefore, wise to suspend judgment about the presence of related psychiatric or psychological problems until sobriety has occurred.

During the stabilization phase of treatment, the acute abstinence syndrome alters and distorts behavior and personality. In cases of severe psychiatric disorder, there will be a nontypical response to the stabilization period. These nontypical responses should be noted and carefully evaluated, but unless the condition is placing the person's sobriety in risk, diagnosis and initial treatment should be suspended until the person has stabilized.

In many instances, however, severe psychiatric illness will interfere with the patient's ability to maintain treatment. The psychiatric problem will develop and the person will leave against medical advice. If this is the case, it is important to get a psychiatric evaluation and use appropriate medications to stabilize the patient. A psychiatric consultant should be identified who understands the disease concept of alcoholism but who is also skilled in psychodiagnosis. It is also helpful to identify a psychologist who is skilled in psychological testing, but who also understands alcoholism and the unique differences in standard psychological test scores that occur with alcoholic patients.

The treatment for the coexisting psychiatric or personality disorder should occur in parallel with treatment for alcoholism. The role of the psychiatrist or psychologist is to stabilize the patient's psychiatric or psychological disorder and to cooperate with the alcoholism counselor in setting up a course of treatment that allows stabilization from alcoholism along with treatment of the psychiatric disorder. The job of the alcoholism counselor is to stabilize the person's alcoholism by establishing a strong, structured recovery program. The counselor's job is then to consult with the psychologist or psychiatrist to interface the ongoing alcoholism counseling with the ongoing needs of psychotherapy so that the person can learn how to be comfortably sober while resolving all related life issues.

SITUATIONAL LIFE PROBLEMS

From time to time there are major or minor situational crises that create problems that require special action to protect sobriety. Death or separation, job or financial or family crisis can create stress and a distraction from the recovery program that may mark a point of transition from the recovery process to the relapse process that goes unnoticed because of preoccupation with the situation or problem. These times of crisis are especially difficult if alcohol has been used as a means of coping at such times in the past.

There are life-transition periods that most adults encounter, whether or not they are alcoholic, that require adjustment and may increase anxiety. The alcoholic may find these transition periods especially difficult and need additional support during these times. The transition from childhood to adulthood; the experience of leaving home for the first time, getting married, starting a family; the transition into middle age, children leaving home, watching the next generation move into adult life roles; the adjustment to retirement. These are all periods of change and anxiety that can trigger a relapse dynamic.

It is easy to forget that recovering alcoholics are normal human beings. As such they are vulnerable to sudden and unanticipated life changes. They often need to make major life changes in order to pursue an effective program of recovery and an effective program of living. Many times alcoholics receive no instruction in how to engage in positive or productive life changes.

When a crisis is severe the patient may need special counseling — grief counseling, family counseling, job counseling, premarital counseling — and special support systems to provide stabilization and support through the crisis and to maintain the structure of the recovery program.

Part Two

RELAPSE PREVENTION

RELAPSE PREVENTION PLANNING

Most relapse in alcoholism is unnecessary. It stems from ignorance — ignorance of past history, ignorance of the warning signs, and ignorance of the techniques for intervening should the warning signs of relapse develop.

Proper relapse prevention planning can instill in the alcoholic, and the people concerned about him, a deep sense of security. All involved can know that they are systematically doing what is necessary to avert relapse. They can develop a check list of the early warning signs and a master action plan for interrupting the relapse dynamic once it appears. As a result, they can be confident, and realistically so, that recovery is following a successful course.

Proper action on the part of the alcoholic and the key people in his life can prevent or interrupt relapse before the consequences become tragic. Planning for relapse minimizes its destructive potential. The alcoholic can utilize intervention skills at any time before drinking becomes out of control if he is prepared to recognize and understand the relapse process.

The alcoholic is ultimately responsible for all behavior and decisions that accompany relapse. He pays most heavily for relapse. Many persons relapse because they do not understand the process and do not know what types of behavior change are necessary to prevent it. Many therapists contribute directly to relapse by failing to thoroughly educate their patients about the relapse process and ways to avoid it. Proper intensive education prior to relapse increases the level of responsibility with which the patient is able to manage the relapse potential of his illness.

The relapse prevention plan is a protocol designed to reduce the risk of relapse in the alcoholic through a process of education, self-exploration, and action planning that involves the alcoholic and those people significant in his life.

The development of a relapse prevention plan is an essential part of the treatment process. The important people in the alcoholic's life should be informed of the potential for relapse and of their responsibility to take appropriate action if the patient demonstrates early warning signs.

Relapse prevention planning works most effectively with patients who have been previously treated for alcoholism and have failed to maintain long-term sobriety. Treatment occurs in the mind of the patient. Because a patient has been through a treatment program for alcoholism does not mean the treatment process has been initiated. For a person to have initiated treatment he must have come to a personal recognition that he is suffering from alcoholism, recognized that total abstinence is necessary for long-term recovery, and made a commitment to a structured recovery program. If these three steps have not occurred, the patient needs to receive basic alcoholism treatment services prior to participating in a relapse prevention planning process. Unless the patient believes that he is alcoholic and can no longer use alcohol, a relapse prevention plan cannot work.

The alcoholic will not identify with the standard relapse warning signs unless he has attempted a period of self-imposed abstinence. The warning signs only emerge as the alcoholic struggles with an attempt to implement a recovery program and maintain total abstinence from alcohol. Without this conscious struggle to achieve a comfortable sobriety, the relapse signs will not be apparent to him as he goes through self-inventory.

The relapse prevention planning process is an adjunct to alcoholism treatment, not a substitute. Relapse prevention planning is simply a method of constructing a fence between the alcoholic and his first drink. The goal of this planning is to make it more difficult for the patient to take a drink than it is to participate in an ongoing program of recovery. Once the relapse prevention plan is established, the presence of that plan will help ensure enough sober time for him to begin to benefit from other aspects of treatment.

Relapse prevention planning is a process that should become an integral part of the treatment for any patient who has attempted previous sobriety and failed. The process can be adapted to work in individual counseling, group counseling, inpatient and outpatient and aftercare settings. It can be presented in patient education sessions or form the basis of in-depth counseling. The relapse prevention plan is a flexible tool that can be utilized by counselors working in a variety of settings.

The outcome of successful relapse prevention planning should be a sober alcoholic who is comfortable in sobriety and knowledgeable of his relapse warning signs, has an action plan to interrupt those warning signs should they develop, and has a problem list that can launch him on a successful course of counseling. The

steps of relapse prevention planning are:
1. Stabilization.
2. Assessment.
3. Patient Education.
4. Warning Sign Identification.
5. Review Of The Recovery Program.
6. Inventory Training.
7. Interruption Of The Relapse Dynamic.
8. Involvement Of Significant Others.
9. Follow-up And Reinforcement.

STABILIZATION

Any alcoholic who returns to drinking is in a crisis. Even if the patient appears calm and collected, you can be certain that he is not. He is scared, embarrassed, and guilt ridden. There may be a variety of life crises that have developed as a result of the relapse or the pre-relapse behavior.

The family and other concerned persons are also in crisis. The relapse disrupts the entire social network. As a result, these people are upset and not functioning normally. They may be frightened, angry, and hurt, or they may experience a bombardment of different feelings. If the family is to be a part of the relapse prevention planning process, they must become involved in a stabilization process along with the relapsed patient.

Don't forget that the alcoholic and his family are masters at denial and that most denial is an unconscious process. The patient and family may not recognize that they are in crisis, and they may have a high investment in convincing the treatment personnel that no crisis exists. But it is impossible to relapse to active alcoholism without disrupting individual and family functioning.

The first step to any relapse prevention planning process is to assure that the patient and his family have been stabilized from the most recent relapse. To assure proper stabilization, the impact of the relapse must be assessed. If the patient is not stable, a treatment plan must be developed that will assure the appropriate support until stabilization can occur. A patient is stabilized when he is in sufficient control of his physical, psychological, behavioral, and social processes that he feels sure that he will not immediately (within the next 24 hours) take a drink. If a patient believes that he may take a drink within the next 24 hours, he is not stable. A protocol for stabilization, which would probably include detoxification in a controlled environment, should be initiated prior to any attempt at relapse prevention planning.

The patient must recognize his need for help. He must be willing to accept treatment in a controlled environment if necessary. After the initial relapse, the patient will have a very strong tendency to minimize the damage and to overestimate his ability to stabilize himself through will power or self-regulated or self-monitored efforts.

It is best to be skeptical of the patient's ability to control his own behaviors until he has established a track record of at least two to five days of total abstinence. Denial factors may cause a person to lie about current drug use. He may be abstaining from alcohol but be using other mood-altering drugs. Therefore, admission into a controlled environment can be very helpful to assess his true condition.

Relapse prevention planning can, and should, begin with detoxification. Following detoxification, the relapse prevention planning process should be continued into inpatient or outpatient care. The sooner the patient begins to examine the concept of relapse and his past relapse history, the less likely he will be to reestablish and fixate upon his old denial systems and rationalizations.

During the period immediately after a relapse, a patient is most receptive to new information. He has failed and has become willing to accept help to correct his failure. He has also been neurologically disorganized by the relapse and the onset of withdrawal. He is scared and confused and is looking for answers. If he doesn't receive solid information immediately, he will begin creating his own answers. In most cases these answers will be part of the denial system that directly contributed to the relapse in the first place. It is imperative that he be provided new information that can take the place of old rationalizations and inaccurate information.

Remember that relapse prevention planning begins during the stabilization period. It begins not only in the process of giving the patient specific information about relapse, but most importantly, it begins in the attitude of the therapist.

It is important that the patient be supported in his efforts toward ongoing recovery and given the message that relapse is no reason for embarrassment. He must be told in no uncertain terms that his first job is to recover from the immediate damage so that he can figure out what went wrong and learn how to correct it. He must develop hope and a belief that he can learn from the experience so that he never has to repeat this failure. Avoid confrontation early in stabilization.

Strong confrontation increases the patient's stress level. The confrontation that should be used during the stabilization period is called *directive self-confrontation*. Self-confrontation occurs when the patient recognizes the inconsistencies in his own behavior. Directive self-confrontation occurs when the patient is guided through an educational process or a clinical interview to examine himself and comes to recognize that his own thoughts are illogical or inconsistent with the reality of his behavior.

Encourage verbalization, ventilation, reality testing, and problem solving in a supportive environment. Don't underestimate the ability of the patient to become immediately involved in his own recovery. Even if he is extremely shaky or confused, he can begin taking immediate and positive steps to stabilize himself and begin sorting out the impact of his previous relapse. The sooner he takes responsibility for his own recovery, the stronger the relapse prevention plan will be.

Provide support and reassurance. The thing the patient needs is supportive human contact. He must know there are people around who understand him and who care about him. He must be aware that he is not being judged or condemned because he has relapsed. As he comes to recognize that other people believe in him in spite of the relapse, he can begin to believe in himself.

Provide positive support and encouragement for entering ongoing treatment. When a patient asks, "Why did I relapse?" the appropriate answer is, "You relapsed because you failed to do everything necessary to stay sober." If a patient fails to do everything necessary to stay sober, it means that at some point he failed to complete necessary steps in treatment. The need for ongoing and long-term treatment must be strongly emphasized and encouraged.

The patient needs an environment that will support initial abstinence, that is free of the availability of alcohol and drugs, and that has resources to treat withdrawal symptoms and related medical problems should they emerge.

Many patients may lose control of their judgment and suffer from severe alcohol cravings. It is helpful, therefore, to put the patient into a controlled environment protected from the availability of drugs and alcohol. Don't hesitate to utilize blood-alcohol or drug screening of urine samples as an objective method of determining that the patient has achieved abstinence from alcohol and other drugs.

Be sure that you recognize the patient's need for immediate stabilization. Very often a relapse can be interrupted if the person is hospitalized for a period of 2 to 5 days for immediate detoxification. To overestimate the patient's ability to cope with the stress brought about by the relapse can cause many patients to fail to maintain abstinence.

Remember that elevated stress causes the post acute withdrawal syndrome (PAW) to become worse. The higher the stress, the more confused and emotionally impaired the patient will become and the more dysfunctional his memory will be. Stress needs to be lowered so he can regain control of his thought processes, emotional processes, and memory.

The patient who has relapsed is going to be extremely upset with himself and might enter into a period of depression. Depression should always be considered as a possible indication of suicidal ideation. The recently relapsed patient is always depressed even when he doesn't show it. Therefore, every patient who has recently relapsed should be considered as a suicide risk until an assessment determines that the risk is not present. In assessing suicide risk, ask a series of very general and nonthreatening questions and progress to address the suicide issue directly. For example: Have you been feeling frustrated or apprehensive about your life lately? Has life been difficult for you? Does it ever become so difficult that at times you feel that life is not worth living? When you feel that life is not worth living, do you ever think it might be better to end it all or to get away from everything? Have you ever thought of killing yourself? Have you ever developed a plan of how to do it? Have you ever acted upon the plan? Have you ever attempted to kill yourself? Do you presently have a plan for killing yourself if certain things happen?

If he has had thoughts about suicide, he should be taken seriously and a suicide intervention should be done. Express concern for the patient's well-being and express strongly that you do not want him to kill himself. This should not be an injunction that "you can't" but rather, "I don't want you to because the world would really lose something valuable." Instill hope by assuring him that, while you know that he doesn't feel like living right now, you also know that that feeling will pass. Make a contract with him that he will not attempt to harm himself without talking to you first. Make a ritual of the contract — get a firm promise, put it on paper, shake hands on it. If the patient has a specific suicide plan, protective measures should be taken.

In order to effectively stabilize the relapsed patient, it is necessary to determine whether the relapse is therapeutic or nontherapeutic.

STABILIZATION FROM A THERAPEUTIC RELAPSE

A therapeutic relapse is one that increases the chances of full recovery. It is usually short term and low consequence in nature. The end result is that the patient learns the undeniable fact that he is alcoholic and cannot drink. He identifies specific issues that have contributed to the relapse that he probably would have been unable to identify without the learning experience.

Many patients have therapeutic relapses that are short term and low consequence and that provide valuable knowledge about ongoing recovery as well as positive motivation for renewed treatment.

The stabilization needs of the patient who has had a therapeutic relapse are significantly different from the patient who has had a nontherapeutic relapse. In stabilizing the patient who has experienced the therapeutic relapse, it is important to assess with him the damage. The patient tends to exaggerate the damage and often believes the relapse has undone all of his hard work and the positive gains accomplished in recovery. If he has experienced a therapeutic relapse, this is not true.

The therapy team must help him overcome the

mistaken belief that he must start all over again. He has made many positive gains in treatment that have not been undone. The relapse has actually been a growth step, and the patient will walk away having accelerated the recovery process. Relapse is often a very effective teacher. The patient can learn lessons that he could never learn in any other way.

It is important to establish a plan to assist the patient in managing normal feelings associated with the therapeutic relapse. These feelings are confusion, disorientation, helplessness, embarrassment, guilt, and a desire to isolate or run away from the relapse and ongoing treatment. As soon as the person is stable, he must reinitiate a heavily structured sobriety plan for a period of three to five months. This sobriety plan needs to be carefully monitored and enforced.

The patient needs to develop or update his relapse prevention plan based on what he has learned from relapse. But most importantly, he must learn to move beyond the relapse experience and return to other developmental issues that are impacting upon his sobriety. He has relapsed because he has neglected some important developmental task in his recovery.

STABILIZATION FROM A NONTHERAPEUTIC RELAPSE

A nontherapeutic relapse is one that makes recovery more difficult. It is of such a long-term nature that the old alcohol thinking and behavioral habits return and are reinforced. It can also be a short-term relapse that results in serious damage to physical health, thought and emotional process, and to the ability to regulate behavior or social structure.

The nontherapeutic relapse has very serious consequences. Once it has been diagnosed, it is often helpful to plan initial stabilization as if this were the patient's first approach to treatment. The patient must be stable enough to understand the treatment plans that are used if he is to benefit from them. He must also be reminded that acute intoxication and acute alcohol withdrawal can be life threatening. The recovery of the patient is never helped by placing him in life-threatening risk.

It is therefore important to evaluate the patient's state of intoxication or withdrawal at the time he approaches the therapist for help and to arrange appropriate treatment for detoxification.

He should be encouraged to learn the lesson of nontherapeutic relapse. This lesson is, "I have done something seriously wrong. I have failed to follow through on treatment recommendations, and as a result, I am seriously ill and in a great deal of physical and personal pain. My first job is to reduce the current crisis and my current level of pain to the point that I can figure out what problems caused the relapse and what I can do to prevent these problems from resurfacing and destroying my sobriety in the future." After the patient is stabilized and has reinitiated a relapse prevention plan, he must establish a new contract for ongoing treatment.

ASSESSMENT

After the patient has been stabilized, the next step is to

complete a thorough assessment. The areas that need to be assessed are as follows:

1. Assessment Of The Presenting Problems. In assessing the presenting problems, the therapist is actually completing the first phase of treatment which is to accomplish the tasks associated with the motivational crisis. The patient must come to understand the exact nature of the crisis that has evolved as a result of his relapse and the exact nature of the complications that activated the relapse dynamic.

2. Assessment Of The Current Relapse Dynamic. It is of critical importance that the patient examine in detail the exact sequence of events that unfolded from the time he began his previous period of sobriety until the time he relapsed and went into treatment. He will find this very difficult to do. As he attempts to fill in the exact sequence of events, he will find that he has great difficulty in remembering all the details of that time period. This is because relapse warning signs have become activated during this period. The activation of relapse warning signs is not a conscious process. The person does not know that they exist. If he does temporarily become aware of them, he soon forgets. As a result, he has large blank spaces or gaps in his memory of the period of time between initial abstinence and his return to drinking.

Through structured interviewing and directive questioning, he can be forced to reconstruct and resurface these events of which he is unaware. This is accomplished by asking him to begin with the initiation of previous treatment and give a detailed and chronological sequence of events that led to the resumption of drinking.

It is also helpful during this period of time to involve the significant people who can provide information that may help fill in the blank spaces or clarify inaccurate, contradictory, or vague information.

3.   *Assessment Of The Relapse History.* The purpose of assessing the relapse history is to determine if the patient is making overall progress in his treatment or if there is a general decline in the effectiveness of treatment. Relapse is not always a sign of treatment failure. If a patient shows a relapse history that indicates longer periods of sobriety, followed by relapses that are of shorter duration and lower consequence, the patient is, in fact, following a recovery process. For many persons suffering from alcoholism, a series of relapses is a necessary and normal part of the recovery process. It is important, however, to determine if the relapse history is improving or degenerating.

This is accomplished by documenting the date that the patient perceived the onset of his own alcoholism; the date at which he first sought outside help in order to recover; the causative factor that prompted the first request for help; the type of help or treatment received; the outcome of that attempt for help or treatment; the date of each actual return to drinking; the duration of controlled use, if any, that occurred when he returned to alcohol use; the severity and duration of episodes of loss of control; the date that drinking was terminated; the method the patient used to terminate the alcohol use; aspects of previous treatment that the patient felt were effective and aspects that he felt were ineffective.

4. Assessment Of The Level Of Treatment Completion. The level of treatment completion is assessed by referring to the developmental phases of recovery and using these as a guideline to help a patient to explore his previous progress in treatment. It is necessary to probe into the details of the patient's recovery to identify the specific recovery tasks that he has failed to complete earlier. Remember that the most common cause of relapse is treatment incompletion. If the exact treatment tasks that were neglected can be identified, a treatment plan can be established that will allow the patient to successfully complete those treatment tasks and avoid relapse in the future.

5. Assessment Of The Factors Complicating Recovery. This is achieved by reviewing with the patient the complicating factors that interfere with a successful recovery process. It is often helpful to use objective testing to determine if any of these complicating factors are currently present in the patient's lifestyle.

6. Assessment Of The Patient's Personality Style. The personality style determines the patient's way of coping with sobriety-based symptoms and complicating factors. The patient needs to identify which of the personality styles — extremely dependent, extremely independent, counterdependent, or functionally dependent — he utilized in his previous period of abstinence and recognize the steps necessary to develop a functionally independent personality style.

In assessing the patient's style of coping with the recovery process and with complicating factors, it is necessary to consider the possibility of multiple diagnosis. Often a patient has significant psychiatric illness that interferes with the recovery process. This can usually be detected early in treatment. If a multiple diagnosis is suspected, the patient should be referred for appropriate diagnosis and, if psychiatric disorders are confirmed, a course of parallel treatment that addresses both the alcoholism and the psychiatric illness needs to be initiated.

PATIENT EDUCATION

The patient must understand the relapse process if he is to recognize it and be able to interrupt it. Patient education is the process of instilling within him the information that is necessary to understand the process of relapse and apply that information to his own personal history and current life situation.

What does the patient need to know about relapse and recovery? A workable patient education model will include the following basic content components:

1. The recovery process — a developmental model of recovery.
2. The sobriety-based symptoms of alcoholism.
3. The factors complicating recovery.
4. The personality styles or personal responses that contribute to relapse and recovery.
5. The relapse dynamic, including the relapse warning

signs.
6. The relapse prevention planning process.

The exact content that the patient needs to be taught is covered elsewhere in this manual under those topic areas. Informational content is only part of the educational process, however. The person must also engage in a process of emotional learning and skills training if the educational process is to be complete.

The basic steps in processing any of the informational content components pertaining to relapse prevention are as follows:

1. Contracting For Review Of The Contract Component. Make an agreement with the patient to review the specific content component. In obtaining this contract, make a strong connection between the content component to be reviewed and the immediate issues that the patient is motivated to work on in treatment.

2. Patient Note Taking. Establish a contract with the patient to take notes as the content component is reviewed. Note taking aids learning. It is also a good test for patient motivation. When the patient begins taking notes, he is forced to translate the information into his own words.

3. Review Of The Content Component. Review the exact content component with the patient. This normally takes the form of a mini-lecture and includes drawing diagrams and telling stories that can bring the content to life. Have a specific and clear diagram that illustrates each of the content components. This is particularly helpful with alcoholics because of the damaged areas of brain functioning. When working with the alcoholic, a picture is truly worth a thousand words. It is also helpful to have memorable stories and numerous examples that depict a point. The alcoholic must have concrete and hard-hitting examples if he is to understand and remember the specific information that he needs in order to avert a future relapse.

4. Patient Reconstruction Of The Content Component.   Ask the patient to put away his notes and remove from view the diagrams constructed. Then ask him to reconstruct the content component and draw the diagram that has just been drawn. It is expected that at this point he will not remember the exact diagram. Review the content component point by point while instructing him how to draw the diagram and asking him to repeat back and translate into personal experience each specific portion. It is important for him not only to remember your examples but also to create his own examples and relate them to his personal relapse history.

5. Evaluating The Outcome Of Patient Education. After the educational process is complete for each content component, it is necessary to evaluate what the patient has learned. This can be accomplished by following these steps:

Elicit exact recall: Ask the patient to "explain to me exactly what I have explained to you."

Elicit translated recall: Ask the patient to "explain the information by putting it into other words that you are comfortable with."

Elicit examples: Ask the patient to "give an example or tell a story that demonstrates this concept." The example or the story can be real or imaginary. It can pertain to the patient, or it can pertain to someone else.

Elicit personal meaning: Ask the patient, "What does this information mean to you?"

This can be a time-consuming process, but unless the patient truly understands and integrates the developmental model of recovery, the sobriety-based symptoms of alcoholism, the factors complicating recovery, the personality styles that contribute to recovery and relapse, the relapse process, and relapse prevention planning, he will be unable to put these practices into place in his life.

WARNING SIGN INDENTIFICATION

Each person has a unique set of personal warning signs of relapse. These are signals that he gives to himself that tell him that he is in risk of drinking. Relapse warning sign identification is the step of relapse prevention planning that assists the patient in developing a list of *personalized warning signs.* This is the most critical phase of relapse prevention planning and the most difficult. The entire outcome of relapse prevention counseling is based upon the development of concrete and easily recognized personal warning signs that indicate that the patient is in danger.

The patient will initially have difficulty identifying warning signs from previous relapses because these warning signs have developed on an unconscious level. It is therefore important for him to go through a structured process of reviewing his relapse dynamic in detail and of finding the words that can describe the exact symptoms that developed.

The primary task in relapse warning sign identification is teaching the patient the skills of self-evaluation, self-disclosure, and receiving critical and constructive feedback from others. It is also important that he learn to reality test the feedback that he receives from those around him. The significant others involved in the alcoholic's life are often suffering from coalcoholism. Their feedback can often be inaccurate. The alcoholic must learn how to listen to what other people have to say and use the resource of his counselor and his AA sponsor to test that information for accuracy.

The basic steps involved in assisting someone in developing a list of personalized warning signs are as follows:

1. Review Of Warning Signs. Review with the patient the list of thirty-seven warning signs of relapse. Be sure he has an opportunity to read the summary title and descriptive statement of each relapse warning sign out loud. Then ask him to translate that warning sign into other words that are more meaningful to him. If the patient is incapable of explaining the warning sign in other words, he probably doesn't understand it and cannot use it as a tool for self-evaluation.

In a group setting, the warning signs can be reviewed simply by having each person read the summary title and descriptive statement of each one. Each person in the group reads one warning sign until all have been reviewed. After each person reads the warning sign, he then translates it into his own words.

In reviewing the warning signs, the patient should be provided with many concrete examples and stories that illustrate how it operates. The patient should be asked to identify situations in his own life, or situations that have occurred with people that he knows, that dramatize that particular warning sign.

2.   Selection Of Priority Warning Signs. After the entire list has been reviewed, the patient should be asked to select three to five warning signs that he believes apply to him.

3.   Construction Of Summary Titles.   A summary title is a word or a short phrase that captures the general meaning of a relapse warning sign. Once a person has identified a sign from the relapse chart, he translates it into his own words. The first step of doing this is having him construct a summary title that is meaningful to him and that he will be able to easily remember. For example, he may pick warning sign number three — adamant commitment to sobriety. As his summary title he might write, "Swearing I'll never drink again." This phrase is far more meaningful to him than "adamant commitment to sobriety" and will be more easily remembered.

If he identifies with relapse warning sign number seven

— impulsive behavior — he may describe it as "suddenly acting crazy." Or he may describe it as "doing unpredictable things." Again, these phrases have far more meaning to him than "impulsive behavior" and will be far more readily remembered in a self-inventory process.

4. Construction Of Descriptive Statements. A descriptive statement is a brief paragraph that defines and describes the exact meaning of a summary title. This can be readily explained by asking the patient to pretend that he is engaged in a twenty-five words or less contest. His job is to write a brief paragraph of twenty-five words or less that explains the meaning of the summary title he has constructed. For example, he may write, "Swearing I'll never drink again: I make a promise to myself that I will never ever take another drink for the rest of my life."

If the personalized warning sign is "suddenly acting crazy," the patient may explain this by describing, "On Friday nights I'll suddenly get fed up and disgusted with being at home, and I'll just go out and wander the streets for no reason at all." Or he may report, "I'll be at work and suddenly I'll be fed up and I'll just walk off the job or start arguing with people for no reason at all."

The important part of descriptive statement construction is getting the patient to identify concrete and observable manifestations of the warning sign. This should involve specific thoughts that he has, specific emotions and body sensations that he experiences, observable situations that he finds himself in, or observable reactions of others to his behavior. A well-defined summary title and descriptive statement will involve all of these. Here is a good example. *"Suddenly Acting Crazy:* I begin to feel trapped, helpless and useless. My stomach tightens up and I clench my teeth. Other people don't understand me and tend to start criticizing me and I say to myself, What's the use? Why bother with it all anyway? I then stop doing what I'm doing and try to get away, but I feel I have no place to go. So I just wander the streets and maybe stop by a bar or two or go to a movie by myself just to try and get control of myself."

This particular warning sign is very concrete. There are specific self-talk statements that the person makes in his own head that he can notice. There are specific statements that describe the emotional state that goes on at the time the warning sign occurs. There are observable behaviors that other people engage in that he can see. There are also concrete observable behaviors that the patient uses that can be recognized.

It is the concrete and specific identification of self-talk statements, emotional reactions, body sensations, high risk situations, reactions of other persons, and personal behaviors that set the stage for identifying specific warning signs.

5. Assignment Of Accuracy Rating. Ask the patient how accurate the statement is on a scale of 1 to 10. Have him put the accuracy rating beside the statement.

6. Experiential Processing. Once this summary title and descriptive statement is constructed, have the person do two mental exercises using that specific warning sign as the focal point. The first mental exercise is to vividly recall a past situation in which that warning sign was a problem. This is accomplished by helping the patient to achieve a deeply relaxed state through the use of a brief relaxation exercise. You then ask him to remember vividly, and in detail, a situation in which that warning sign has been operative in his life. You ask him to see all that there is to see about that situation. You ask him to hear all that there is to hear about the situation and to feel all that there is to feel about the situation. Ask him to remember specific sights, sounds, textures, colors. Ask him to look closely at the people who were involved and try to remember the clothes they were wearing, try to see in their eyes, try to sense the atmosphere in the room while the event was occurring. The more vividly you can reconstruct a situation, the more helpful it will be.

The second mental exercise is to have the person vividly create a situation in the future in which this warning sign is likely to be a problem or a threat to his ongoing sobriety. *Every alcoholic secretly carries within him a fantasy of what his next relapse will be like.* Every alcoholic carries within him the secret knowledge of what it will take for him to begin drinking again. In accomplishing the experiential processing of a potential future event related to a relapse warning sign, these hidden self-fulfilling prophecies can be raised to a conscious level and the patient can become acutely aware of the situations that place him in high risk of relapse.

If the experiential processing of the past occurrences and future projections of each relapse warning sign is successfully completed, the patient will have a catharsis (a change in feeling), an insight (a change in understanding), and a motivation to change his behavior. This is the goal of relapse prevention planning — to assist the person in changing his unconscious responses to the presence of relapse warning signs. The goal is to establish a new unconscious reaction to the presence of a warning sign. Instead of accepting it as normal, the patient's unconscious mind needs to trigger a warning or a red alert that says this is dangerous, this is abnormal.

7. *Clarification And Corrections.* If the experiential processing has been successfully completed, the patient's perception of the warning sign itself may change. At this point, review the summary title and descriptive statement word for word and ask if he believes that it is 100% accurate or if he could change the exact description to make it more accurate or more specific.

There are several problems that are typically present in the construction of relapse warning signs. The patient often selects what he believes to be relapse warning signs that, in fact, *do not necessarily reflect risk of relapse.* An example of this is a patient who identifies arguing with his wife as a warning sign when, in reality, he only argues with his wife after he has returned to drinking. The real warning sign was his anger toward his wife and his unwillingness or inability to express that anger unless drunk.

The signs may be *too general and vague.* The patient may identify a warning sign, but it is not clearly and concretely described. In order for the warning signs to be an effective tool of relapse prevention, they must be specific and concrete. You must be able to take a picture of it, make a movie of it, or put it in a box. If you can't do one of these three things, they are not concrete and specific enough.

REVIEW OF THE RECOVERY PROGRAM

By developing a list of personalized warning signs, the person is able to recognize when things are going wrong. He has a checklist of problem indicators that tells him he is in trouble. If this is all he has, he can only think negatively about his recovery and continuously check for problem areas.

He should counterbalance his search for relapse warning signs by looking for positive indicators of recovery. This occurs through review of the recovery program or inventory of positive progress in recovery. The basic way in which this is accomplished is as follows:

1. Review Of The Recovery Program. Review in detail the person's sobriety program, the recovery skills that he has developed, and the attitudes and personality dynamics that were present prior to his previous relapse. By doing this, he can identify both the positive aspects and the negative or self-defeating aspects of that recovery program.

2. Development Of A New Recovery Program. The patient should redesign his recovery program based upon the lessons learned by the previous failure, a program that will offset the weaknesses or problems that he has identified. His previous recovery program did not work. If he attempts sobriety using the same recovery program, the outcome will probably be the same — he will relapse. It only makes sense, if you have tried something once and it hasn't worked, to try something different.

3. Reinforcement. The person should know how to structure personal and interpersonal reinforcement for his new recovery program. In other words, he must have a way of telling himself that he is doing a good job on a daily basis and inviting others to give him positive support and encouragement. Without this continuous personal and interpersonal support, he will become lax in implementing the program on a daily basis.

4. Monitoring Until The Sobriety Program Becomes Habitual. It takes eight to twelve weeks for a new behavior to become habitual. Until a behavior or an activity becomes habitual, it takes extra effort to complete the activity. After habituation has occurred, a person will feel comfortable doing the activity, and if he ever neglects doing it, he will feel that something is wrong.

Using this law of habituation, it is very clear to see that the patient needs a structured and monitored program for at least eight to twelve weeks. Once the recovery program has become habitual, the extent of the monitoring can be decreased.

INVENTORY TRAINING

Any successful recovery program involves a daily

inventory. The alcoholic must learn to challenge himself and his day-to-day living patterns. In relapse prevention planning the alcoholic is asked to design a special inventory system to determine if he is in the process of recovery or in the process of relapse. He develops ways to incorporate this inventory system into his day-to-day living. He now has tools available that will enable him to look for his strengths and weaknesses and monitor his daily sobriety plan.

The daily inventory needs to revolve around positive recovery indicators, negative aspects of recovery, and personal responses and attitudes toward recovery and the need for treatment. Am I doing everything necessary to recover? Am I completing all the necessary components of my recovery program? Are there any warning signs that are developing in my life? Do I recognize that I am alcoholic? Do I recognize that I am in need of a daily recovery program? Am I beginning to feel resentful or uneasy about my daily program of recovery? Is there a part of me that is beginning to believe that I no longer need to pursue a daily recovery program?

The following steps will assist in instructing the patient in taking a daily inventory.

1.   *Patient Instruction In The Importance Of Inventory Training.* The patient must be instructed about the importance of daily inventory in the recovery process. The patients who conduct a daily inventory are the patients who recover over the long term.

If even one relapse warning sign is present, personal denial mechanisms may be reactivated. It is not uncommon for a person to recognize the presence of a relapse warning sign and then do nothing about it. When asked why he did nothing, his usual response is, "I just didn't think it was that important."

The patient must recognize that any relapse warning sign is serious because it can be the first step toward taking a drink or physical or emotional collapse.

2. *Instruction In Specific Methods Of Inventory.* In order to practice an effective inventory, the person must establish a daily time and place to complete the inventory. This needs to become habitual. It is recommended that the recovering alcoholic establish two daily inventory rituals. The first should occur in the morning. He should clear five to ten minutes to read the daily entry in the Twenty-Four Hour A Day Book and to briefly outline his personal goals and objectives for the day on a sheet of paper. The goal of this inventory is to become physically and psychologically prepared to meet the challenges of the day and maintain a comfortable sobriety. Am I prepared physically and emotionally for this day? What have I done or will I do specifically before becoming involved in my daily routine to assist me in this preparation? What are my major goals or objectives for the day?

The second ritual should occur in the evening just prior to bedtime. The purpose is to review the tasks of the day, identify the positives and negatives that occurred, reinforce the positive elements, and plan methods for improving the negative elements. As I review my recovery program, did I fulfill all of the commitments I made to myself? As I review the daily events, am I aware of any problem areas or shortcomings that need to be corrected tomorrow? As I review my personalized list of warning signs, are any present in my life? If so, what have I done today to correct those situations? Is there any unfinished business of the day that needs to be completed before I can rest comfortably and in good conscience?

The person should begin the evening inventory with a quiet time of at least two minutes. During this quiet time, he should concentrate on reviewing the daily activities from the time he got up until the moment of his inventory. Next, he should review his written recovery plan and ask the question, have I complied with all the requirements of my recovery plan today?

Next, he should take out his list of personalized relapse warning signs. He should review these and ask himself if there were any present in the course of the day and if there are any others that should be added to the list.

The patient should ask himself if any traits of the self-defeating personality styles showed themselves during the day. He should also ask himself how he feels about being sober, how he feels about being alcoholic, and how he feels about his need to practice a daily recovery program.

It is helpful if the recovering person documents the results of his daily inventory in a journal or personal log. The process of keeping a journal or log is useful in reviewing progress of recovery and of monitoring for relapse warning signs. The inability to discipline oneself to keep a daily journal of the inventory process may itself be a relapse warning sign. It may be an indication that something is occurring that is too uncomfortable to face.

When instructing a patient about completing a daily

inventory, point out that most successful people are in the habit of doing two inventories per day. This practice is strongly recommended by professional planners, business executives, and sales people. In the morning, plan the day and prepare to meet its challenges. In the evening, review the day and note progress and problems. It is progress we strive for and not perfection.

3. Integrating The Inventory Process Into AA And Professional Counseling. Daily inventory is an integral part of the AA program. The Tenth Step states, "continued to take personal inventory and when we were wrong promptly admitted it."

Applying this step requires taking the daily inventory, evaluating the outcome of the inventory (if necessary with someone else), and recognizing and admitting the wrong.

The final component of a successful inventory process is a regular review of the outcome of the daily inventories with a counselor and/or AA sponsor. It is only when we can confront the realities of our lives in the presence of someone else that we can be truly honest with ourselves. Step 5 in AA reads, "admitted to God, to ourselves, and to another human being the exact nature of our wrongs." It is important that we admit our successes and our failures to another person. It is only when we do this that we can truly face our strengths and our shortcomings and learn how to grow beyond our current limitations. This means acknowledging positive efforts at implementing the recovery program and recognizing the presence of relapse warning indicators.

Relapse warning signs do not occur in isolation. If

there is one relapse warning sign that is obvious, there are probably many others that are hidden from personal view. It is impossible for us to look at our own lives objectively. The person needs to get outside help, talk to his counselor or AA sponsor or someone he trusts who can give objective feedback.

The inventory process should be part of the patient's total AA and professional counseling program. It cannot be isolated or removed from what he is working on in those programs.

INTERRUPTION OF THE RELAPSE DYNAMIC

It is not enough to simply recognize the presence of a relapse warning sign; the patient must take action in order to remove the warning sign from his life. The presence of the relapse dynamic in the life of the alcoholic is not different from the presence of any other problem. It is simply a problem and it can be solved by using the standard problem-solving process. This standard process consists of the following steps:

1. Problem Identification. First you have to identify what is causing the relapse warning signs. What exactly is the problem? The problem may seem simple at first, but as it is examined, many surprising facets may surface.

2. Problem Clarification. Be specific, concrete, and complete. Is this the real problem or is there a more fundamental problem? Is this the only warning sign that is present, or are there other more subtle warning signs?

Remember, a relapse warning sign seldom travels alone.

3. Identification Of Alternatives. How can the relapse dynamic be interrupted? How can positive action be initiated that will remove the relapse warning signs? What are the options that are available for interrupting the relapse dynamic and returning to a recovery dynamic. The options should be listed on a sheet of paper where they can be easily seen. Listing at least five possible solutions or alternatives will give more chance of choosing the best solution and give alternatives as backup plans if the first choice doesn't work.

4. Projected Consequences of Each Alternative. What are the probable consequences or outcomes for each option selected? Three questions should be asked in reference to each option that has been identified: What is the *best* possible result of choosing this alternative? What is the *worst* possible result? What is the *most likely* result?

5. Decision. Which option offers the best probable outcome and seems to be the most reasonable choice or solution? Make a decision to implement the option that seems most likely to be effective in interrupting the relapse process.

6. Action. Once a solution has been selected, a plan is necessary to carry it out. Making a plan answers the question, What am I going to do to interrupt these specific relapse warning signs? A plan is a road map to achieve a goal. Remember, in interrupting the relapse dynamic there must be both long-range goals and short-range goals. A long-range goal is to walk to a store a mile away. A short-range goal is to take the first step. The long-range goal of removing the relapse warning signs must be accomplished by specific activities that will sustain sobriety one day at a time.

Planning and action go hand in hand. Don't just plan — act. Do it! Try it! That's what relapse prevention planning is all about: deciding that you are going to recover and then doing everything necessary to make that recovery possible.

7. Follow-up. As the plan is carried out it must be evaluated for effectiveness. Sharing success with someone else helps to reinforce it. If the plan has failed to interrupt the relapse dynamic, it will be necessary to establish a new and more effective plan.

INVOLVEMENT OF SIGNIFICANT OTHERS

A person cannot recover from alcoholism in isolation. Total recovery involves the help and support of a variety of persons. Relapse prevention is only possible if other people are involved. The recovering person needs to select significant individuals in his life to become involved in the relapse prevention process. These people will be identified as the *intervention network.*

Immediate family members, supportive employers, close personal friends, an AA sponsor, or close friends on the AA program should all be involved in the intervention network.

In general, the intervention network consists of

concerned persons who are committed to the recovery of the person suffering from alcoholism. The patient establishes an intervention network by inviting these people directly and openly into the recovery process. These significant people learn to participate in the patient's recovery plan and learn how to refuse to participate in the relapse process.

It is challenging for these people to become involved. They must make commitments, not only to helping the alcoholic recover, but also to practicing a program of personal recovery. Remember, the disease of alcoholism affects all who are closely involved with it. There are no exceptions. The family members, close personal friends, employers, even fellow associates in Alcoholics Anonymous can be affected by the progressive relapse dynamic.

The members of the intervention network participate in the patient's recovery by encouraging and reinforcing the behaviors that constitute the recovery process. They refuse to participate in the relapse process by confronting or failing to reinforce relapse warning symptoms. They make a commitment to become active participants in the role of enabling recovery rather than relapse. A recovery network can be developed by following these steps:

1. The Identification Of Significant Others. The patient needs to develop a list of all of the people with whom he has routine daily contact. With the help of his therapist or AA sponsor, he needs to select from that list the persons that he thinks would be important in helping him avoid relapse and to request that they become involved in the relapse prevention process.

2. Response Pattern Identification And Evaluation. The goal of this step is to identify how each specific person in the intervention network has responded in the past to the presence of relapse warning signs. The patient should then be asked to identify whether or not the responses to the warning signs contributed to his maintaining the relapse dynamic or encourage dhim to enter into the recovery process. This is the vital question. Were the past responses helpful or were they harmful?

This task is not as easy as it might sound. In order to evaluate the responses of the significant persons to the presence of warning signs, the following exercise may be helpful. First, take several sheets of paper and enter the name of each member of the intervention network at the top of a separate page. There should be one name on the top of each page.

Next, take one sheet at a time and divide it into three columns. Label the first column *Relapse Warning Sign;* label the second column *Past Response;* and label the third column *Assessment.*

Under the column labeled *Relapse Warning Sign,* place the summary titles of the personalized relapse warning signs that were identified earlier. Under the column labeled *Past Response,* write a statement describing the typical past response of that particular person to the presence of the specific warning sign.

Under the column labeled *Assessment,* determine whether this person's past response was productive or counterproductive. A productive response would confront the presence of the warning sign, interrupt it, and encourage and reinforce the patient to reenter the recovery process. A counterproductive response would be one that ignored the symptom, enabled the patient to maintain the symptom, actively supported the symptom, or confronted the symptom in a destructive manner. The end result of a counterproductive response is that the patient is allowed to continue in a relapse dynamic and avoid the logical consequences of his behaviors.

3. Identification Of Alternative Responses. For each counterproductive response that was identified and evaluated in step two, the patient needs to identify alternative responses that would assist him in recognizing that he is in the process of relapse and assist him in altering his behavior so he can reestablish a recover dynamic. The patient needs to identify how he would like each person to respond to the presence of each warning sign that is observed.

It is easy to focus entirely upon the negative aspects in the development of a relapse prevention plan. It is helpful, however, to make some positive plans. For others to be helpful in interrupting relapse they must be able to supportively confront the presence of warning signs without becoming part of the problem and invite the alcoholic into new and more productive behaviors and activities.

The end result should be the development of a preferred list of alternative behaviors. This list should answer the question, How would I want this person to respond to me in the future if I show relapse warning signs? Or how could this person be most helpful to my ongoing sobriety when I am showing warning signs of relapse? An example of a strategy list is presented below:

Person: Nellie (my wife)
Warning Sign: Oversleeping on workday mornings.
Old Response: Nellie would yell and scream at me and get frustrated. After two or three mornings of this, she would simply stop talking to me and stop trying to wake me up.
Preferred Response: Wake me in the morning on time. If I don't get up, remind me fifteen minutes later and then leave me alone. Refuse to cover for me or call in to work for me. If I am late getting up and late for work, talk to me about her concerns in the evening. Bring to my attention any causes for the oversleeping that she may be aware of, such as excessive napping in the evening, going to bed too early, etc.

4. *Establish A Denial Interruption Plan.*   The presence of relapse warning signs is generally unconscious. The patient doesn't recognize the warning signs because he is protected by a very strong denial system. When confronted with the warning sign, the denial system will be activated and the patient will generally refuse to acknowledge that what the other people are telling him is true. The refusal may be, and often is, accompanied by intense anger.

The patient needs to be asked this question: What are other people supposed to do if you deny or refuse to acknowledge the presence of warning signs when they observe the signs and respond in the agreed way? The patient needs to think seriously about this question. What if his denial gets out of control? What if his process of *self-lying* becomes so strong that he denies reality? Remember, the patient in the relapse dynamic often loses control of his judgment and his behavior before he ever takes the first drink. If he is out of control of his judgment and his behavior when he is confronted, he may become extremely angry and resentful and have a tendency to run away from the confrontation.

5. A Relapse Early Intervention Plan. It is a reality that many patients relapse in the course of their recovery. Once this reality is faced, the patient and the significant others can be prepared to take appropriate action should the patient return to drinking.

If the patient were suffering from heart disease and could suddenly become unconscious and die without medication, the family members would learn how to administer the life-saving medication. If there were a member of the family with epilepsy, the family members would learn how to manage seizures. If there is an alcoholic in the family, the family must learn the correct responses should the patient return to alcohol use.

An early intervention plan answers the question: What am I supposed to do if the alcoholic member of my family returns to the use of alcohol or other drugs? The patient needs to be involved in this planning process and needs to tell the family exactly what he wants them to do. Remember that if the patient returns to alcohol or drug use, he will not be reasonable at that time. He may become angry and resentful at the attempts to help. But the intervention is necessary and may save his life.

6. Intervention Network Instruction. The significant

others should become involved in the relapse prevention planning process as a group. The next section of this chapter will be devoted to a detailed discussion about the tasks that must be completed by the intervention network.

THE INTERVENTION NETWORK

The significant others should be involved in the treatment process from the first contact with the treatment center. Ideally, a family member or close friend should accompany the person for his screening interview, and the entire family should be involved in treatment from the first day. Remember that alcoholism is a family disease that affects all family members and all close friends. All persons concerned should come to understand the disease and take an active role in implementing treatment recommendations that are necessary to return the family and social networks back to normal functioning.

A part of this involvement in treatment, especially for the patient who has a previous history of relapse, is to become involved in specialized relapse prevention planning. Following is a description of a relapse intervention network meeting.

1. Recovery/Relapse Education. The person running the meeting will briefly explain the recovery/relapse process to the entire group to be sure that everyone understands the reason for the meeting and the exact problem that is being addressed.

2. Presentation Of Personal Warning Signs. The patient, with the assistance of the counselor, will present to the group his understanding of his personal relapse warning signs. After the presentation, the group will be asked to give the patient critical and supportive feedback. Are the warning signs accurate in the perception of the significant others? Are there any warning signs that the patient has missed that should be added to the list?

3. Presentation Of Previous And Preferred Responses. The patient will next present to each individual member of the intervention network his perception of his past behavior and that person's response to the relapse warning signs. He will state how he would like the person to respond in the future should the same warning signs develop.

After the patient presents his past observations and his preferred future responses, the individual family member will have a chance to comment and the other members present in the meeting will be able to comment and give feedback. The goal is for all persons to have an accurate understanding of what has happened in the past when relapse warning signs have developed and how those situations can be more effectively managed in the future.

4. Denial Interruption Plan. The therapist will next ask the patient the question, "How do you want these people to respond to you if they confront you with the relapse warning signs in the exact way that you have recommended and you refuse to acknowledge the presence of the warning signs?"

Counseling For Relapse Prevention

The group should discuss this. How should they deal with the patient if he is in strong denial when they attempt to bring the relapse warning signs to his attention? What does the patient want the group to do? When sober and thinking clearly the patient will be able to instruct the family in how to get around his denial patterns and be most helpful.

5. Early Intervention Plan. The family needs to discuss openly and honestly the possibility that the patient may return to drinking. What does the patient want the family to do if he begins using alcohol? What are the family members willing to do if they notice that the patient is using alcohol or other drugs or if they have strong suspicions that he is? These are vital questions that must be openly dealt with and discussed in the group.

6. Response Training. If a significant other is going to be helpful to the patient in avoiding relapse, he must learn how to supportively confront the presence of relapse warning signs while inviting the patient to change his behavior and reenter the recovery process. Each family member must make a specific agreement that he will attempt to do these two things if the relapse warning signs develop.

7. Role Playing And Practice. The family members must practice dealing with the recovering patient at his worst. In order to do this, the patient is asked to role play a situation in which he may be showing warning signs and then deny these warning signs. The family members are then to have an actual role play confronting the individual and rehearsing what they would do.

8. A Commitment To Family Recovery. The family is not simply a tool to the alcoholic's recovery. Each family member has his own recovery needs. The recovering person should acknowledge the needs of other family members and make a strong commitment to assist them in their own recovery programs.

Relapse prevention planning can be a strong vehicle towards encouraging all family members to get actively involved in a personal recovery program. All persons who are closely involved with an alcoholic will have issues that need to be resolved as the patient recovers. Many times the significant others are reluctant to become involved in a process to identify and resolve their own problems but are willing to become involved in order to help the patient recover. The intervention network meeting can be an effective method of encouraging the family members to seek the help that they need in their own personal recovery and to work together on issues that affect the family unit.

FOLLOW-UP AND REINFORCEMENT

Relapse prevention planning is not a substitute for treatment. Relapse prevention planning is a specialized procedure that is a first step in treatment for the patient who has difficulty maintaining long periods of sobriety. Its primary goal is to keep the patient away from the use of alcohol and other drugs long enough to allow a program of effective treatment to be implemented. It is therefore vital that the relapse prevention planning process be integrated with other forms of treatment including ongoing involvement with Alcoholics Anonymous or other self-help groups.

After the patient completes formalized treatment, the relapse prevention plan should be integrated with the ongoing maintenance plan. Recovery from alcoholism is a way of life. Since relapse prevention planning is part of the recovery process, it too must become a way of life. Relapse prevention planning is a process that must be practiced until it becomes a habit.

We are all enslaved by our habits. The only freedom we can find is to choose carefully the habits to which we allow ourselves to become enslaved. There is an old cliche that states: There is freedom in structure. This is particularly true for the recovering alcoholic. It is only in the habitual structure of a daily sobriety program that the alcoholic can find freedom from the living death of alcoholism.

There are three steps that must be followed if relapse prevention planning is to become part of an ongoing way of life.

1. Integrating The Relapse Prevention Plan With Alcoholics Anonymous And Other Self-Help Groups. Relapse prevention planning must be done in such a way that it is compatible with the principles and practices of AA and other appropriate support groups that the patient is using to maintain ongoing sobriety.

2. Integrating Relapse Prevention Planning With On-going Treatment For The Patient And The Family. Remember, recovery is a process that requires a period of approximately two years. During this two-year process, the patient will evolve through a variety of phases in his recovery. Each phase carries with it its unique challenges and its unique problems. There are a variety of complicating factors that can emerge at any point in the recovery process. The patient needs treatment in order to overcome these problems.

Alcoholism is a family problem, and all family members require treatment if they are to become a productive family unit again. Each family member should be involved in his own personal program of recovery, and if there are significant family problems, family therapy should be strongly considered.

3. Integrating Relapse Prevention Planning Into The Ongoing Maintenance Plan. After the completion of formalized treatment, ongoing attention to the relapse prevention plan should be given by including it as part of the ongoing aftercare contract.

* * *

One hundred years ago we thought alcohol caused alcoholism. Then we found that alcoholism was a disease. But we thought that it was untreatable. Twenty years ago we believed that an alcoholic couldn't stop drinking until he hit bottom. In recent years the use of intervention technology has demonstrated that this belief was also in error.

Yesterday we believed that the relapse-prone person

was hopeless and could not recover. Today we are beginning to learn that this is not true. The relapse prone are suffering from the sobriety-based symptoms of the disease. As we discover new information about the effects of alcoholism that place a patient in high risk of relapse, we become able to develop a relapse prevention technology that can save millions of lives and untold suffering.

Relapse prevention planning is a new aspect of the alcoholism treatment sciences. This book is not a definitive or final answer. It is more appropriately described as a crude beginning. The major thing we know about relapse is that we don't know a lot about it. It is hoped that this book will encourage other counselors and researchers to document their efforts at preventing relapse and to communicate their findings to one another.

BIBLIOGRAPHY

Alcoholics Anonymous, *Twelve Steps And Twelve Traditions.* New York, Alcoholics Anonymous World Service Inc.,1972.

Armor, D.J.; Pouch, J. Mand Stanbul, H.B.; *Alcoholism and Treatment.* Rand, Santa Monica, California, June, 1976.

Bailey, M.B. and Leach, B., *Alcoholics Anonymous Pathway To Recovery, A Study Of 1,058 Members Of The AA Fellowship In New York City,* The National Council on Alcoholism, Inc., New York, July, 1965.

Bandler, Richard and Grinder, John, *Frogs Into Princes, Neurolinguistic Programming,* Moab, Utah, Real People Press, 1979.

Bandler, Richard and Grinder, John, *The Structure Of Magic.* Palo Alto, California, Science and Behavior Books, 1975.

Bradley, Alan D., *The Psychology Of Memory.* New York, Basic Books, 1976.

Bennet, A.E. et al. Brain Damage from Chronic Alcoholism, The Diagnosis of Intermediate Stage of Alcoholic Brain Disease. *Am. J. Psychiat.* 116, 1960.

Bennet, A.E. *Alcoholism And the Brain.* New York, Stratton Intercontinental Medical Corp., 1977.

Counseling For Relapse Prevention

Birnbaum, Isabel M. and Parker, Elizabeth S. (eds.) *Alcohol And Human Memory.* New Jersey, Lawrence Erlbaum Associates, 1977.

Bourne, Peter G. and Fox, Ruth (eds.) *Alcoholism Progress in Research and Treatment.* New York, Academic Press, 1973.

Budenz, Daniel T., *Relapse To Alcohol/Drug Addiction,* Middleton, Wisconsin, 1979.

Clinebell, Howard J. Jr. *Understanding And Counseling The Alcoholic.* Nashville, Abdington, 1961.

Charalampous, K.D., "Alcohol Related Medical Illness" in *Alcoholism Counseling.* Vol. 1, (ed.) William L. Gideon, Matteson, Illinois, Good and Golden, 1976.

Criteria Committee of the National Council on Alcoholism, "Criteria for the Diagnosis of Alcoholism," *American Journal Of Psychiatry,* 129: 127-135, 1972.

DePalma, N. and Clayton, H.D. Scores of Alcoholics on the 16 Personality Factor Questionnaire. *J. Clin. Psychology.* 14:390-392, 1958.

Fabre, Louis F., "Metabolic and Endocrine Aspects of Alcoholism" in *Alcoholism Counseling,* Vol. 1, (ed.) William L. Gideon, Matteson, Illinois, Good and Golden, 1976.

Farmer, R. Functional Changes During Early Weeks of

Abstinence Measured by the Bender-Gestalt, Quart. J. Stud. Alc. 34-786-796, 1973.

Feinman, L. and Lieber, C.S., 1976, "Liver Disease in Alcoholism," Kissin, B. and Begleiter, H., (eds.) *The Biology Of Alcoholism, Vol. 3: Clinical Pathology.* New York, Plenum Press, 1976.

Glasser, William, *Positive Addiction.* New York, Harper and Row, 1976.

Goodwin, Donald W., *Is Alcoholism Hereditary* New York, Oxford University Press, 1976.

Gordon, David, *Therapeutic Metaphors.* Cupertino, California, Meta Publications, 1978.

Gorski, Terence T. *Denial Patterns: A System For Understanding The Alcoholic's Behavior.* Harvey, Illinois, Ingalls Memorial Hospital, 1976.

Gorski, Terence T., *The Dynamics Of Relapse In The Alcoholic Patient.* Harvey, Illinois, Ingalls Memorial Hospital, 1976.

Gorski, Terence T. and Hannig, H.T., *An Overview OF Alcoholism Consumption And Alcoholism,*Harvey, Illinois, Ingalls Memorial Hospital, 1977.

Gorski, Terence T.; Piontek, Frank A. and Hannig, H.T. *Applications Of Neuropsychology To Alcoholism.* Harvey, Illinois, Ingalls Memorial Hospital, 1977.

Gross, M.M.; Lewis, E. and Begleiter, H. (eds.) *The Biology Of Alcoholism, Vol. 3: Clinical Pathology.* New York, Plenum Press, 1974.

Gross, M.M.; Lewis E. and Hastey, J., Alcohol Acute Withdrawal Syndrome. In Kissin, B. and Begleiter, H. (eds.) *The Biology Of Alcoholism, Vol. 3: Clinical Pathology.* New York, Plenum Press, pp.191-263, 1974.

Hore, B. Factors in Alcoholic Relapse, *British Journal Of Addiction,* 66, p. 88-96, 1971.

Jacobson, George R., *The Alcoholisms: Detection, Diagnosis And Assessment.* New York, Human Sciences Press, 1976.

Jellinek, E.M. *The Disease Concept Of Alcoholism.* New Brunswick, New Jersey, College and University Press, 1960.

Jellinek, E.M. *The Disease Of Alcoholism.* New Haven, College and University Press, 1960.

Johnson, Vernon, *I'll Quit Tomorrow.* New York, Harper and Row, 1973.

Kelly, Patricia and Prince, Bonnie, "Educating Alcoholics in Healthy Nutritional Habits: An Important Aspect of Alcoholism Treatment", 1978. Unpublished.

Kinney, Jean and Leaton, Gwen, *Loosening The Grip.* St. Louis, C.V. Mosby Company, 1974.

Kirsch, G.B. et al. Impaired Abilities in Alcoholics, *Quart. J. Stud. Alc.* 30:383.

Kissin, B. and Begleitter, H. (eds.), *The Biology Of Alcoholism, Vol 3: Clinical Pathology,* New York, Plenum Press, 1974.

Kissin, B.and Begleiter, H. (eds.), *The Biology Of Alcoholism, Vol. 4: Social Aspects Of Alcoholism.* New York, Plenum Press, 1976.

Kissin, B. and Begleiter, H. (eds.), *The Biology Of Alcoholism, Vol. 5: Treatment And Rehabilitation Of The Chronic Alcoholic.* New York, Plenum Press, 1977.

Lezak, Muriel D., *Neuropsychological Assessment.* New York, Oxford University Press, 1976.

Lisansky, E.E. Clinical Research in Alcoholism and the Use of Psychological Tests: A reevaluation. *J. Consult. Psychol.* 32:18-20, 1968.

Milam, James R. and Ketcham, Katherine, *Under The Influence.* Seattle, Washington, Madrona Publishers, 1981.

Miller, Merlene and Gorski, Terence T. *Family Recovery, Growing Beyond Addiction.* Independence, Missouri, Independence Press, 1982.

Miller, Merlene; Gorski, Terence T. and Miller, David K., *Learning To Live Again.* Independence, Missouri,

Counseling For Relapse Prevention

Independence Press, 1982.

Reitan, Ralph M. and Davison, Leslie A., (eds.) *Clinical Neuropsychology: Current Status And Applications.* Washington D.C., V.H. Winson & Sons, 1974.

Rokan, W.P. et al. MMPI Changes in Alcoholics During Hospitalization. *Quart. J. Stud. Alc.* 30 (2):389-401, 1969.

Russell, Elbert W.; Neurenger, Charles and Goldstein, Gerald, *Assessment Of Brain Damage: A Neuropsychological Key Approach.* Wiley - Interscience, 1970.

Sharma, Timothy, "The Pharmacology of Alcohol and the Effects of Alcohol Upon the Systems of the Body" in *Alcoholism Counseling,* Vol. 1, (ed.) William L. Gideon. Matteson, Illinois, Good and Golden, 1976.

Shealy, C. Norman, *The Pain Game.* Millbrae, California, Celestial Arts, 1976.

Smith, J.W. Neurological Disorders in Alcoholism, In Estes, N.J. and Heinemann, M.E., (eds.) *Alcoholism: Development, Consequences and Intervention.*   St. Louis, C.V. Mosby, pp. 109-128, 1977.

Wallgren, Hendrik and Barry, Herbert III, *Actions Of Alcohol Vol. I: Biochemical, Physiological & Psychological Aspects.* New York, 1979.

Wallgren, Hendrick and Barry, Herbert III, *Actions Of Alcohol Vol. II: Chronic And Clinical Aspects.*New York, 1970.

White, W.F. and Porter, T.L., Self-Concept Reports Among Hospitalized Alcoholics During Early Periods of Sobriety, *J. Couns. Psychol.* 13:352:355, 1966.

Witkin, H.A., Psychological Differentiation and Forms of Pathology. *J. Abnorm Psychol.*

TRAINING IN RELAPSE PREVENTION

Relapse prevention planning is a skill that requires training, practice, and supervision. Most agencies are not equipped to effectively train or supervise staff in these methods. Since relapse prevention planning is such a specialty, CENAPS Corporation offers professional training through workshops and inservice training. CENAPS Corporation will also open a Center For Relapse Prevention® within a treatment center or private practice. If an agency opens a Center For Relapse Prevention® , CENAPS Corporation will train and supervise the staff, develop patient care protocols and patient record systems, and link these systems into an applied research network.

For information contact

CENAPS Corporation
P.O. Box 184
Hazel Crest, Illinois
60429
(312) 335-3606

Books, Brochures, and Audiocassettes
ORDER FORM

HERALD HOUSE—INDEPENDENCE PRESS
P.O. BOX HH — 3225 SOUTH NOLAND ROAD
INDEPENDENCE, MO 64055

Qty.	Item No.	Item	Price Ea.	Total Price
		Books:		
____	17-0120-7	Staying Sober	$10.95	$_____
____	17-0136-3	Staying Sober Workbooks	19.95	_____
____	17-0105-3	Learning to Live Again	10.95	_____
____	17-0104-5	Counseling for Relapse Prevention	9.95	_____
____	17-0109-6	Family Recovery, Growing Beyond Addiction	6.00	_____
____	17-0106-1	The Management of Aggression and Violence	6.95	_____
____	17-0164-9	Triad: The Evolution of Treatment	6.00	_____
		Brochures:		
____	17-0111-8	The Relapse Dynamic	.10	_____
____	17-0117-7	The Phases and Warning Signs of Relapse	1.00	_____
____	17-0137-1	Mistaken Beliefs	2.00	_____
		Lecture:		
____	17-0165-7	Do Family of Origin Problems Cause Chemical Addiction?	5.00	_____
		Audiocassettes:		
____	17-0156-8	Addictive Relationships	9.95	_____
____	17-0157-6	Cocaine Craving and Relapse	9.95	_____
____	17-0158-4	Understanding Twelve Steps	36.95	_____
____	17-0139-8	Relaxation by Numbers	7.95	_____
____	17-0140-1	The Phases and Warning Signs of Relapse	7.95	_____

TOTAL COST FOR MERCHANDISE $_____
Please add 10% postage and handling. _____
(Missouri residents only add 5.725% sales tax.) _____
TOTAL $_____

RETAIL ORDERS OF $100.00 OR MORE RECEIVE
A 20 PERCENT DISCOUNT

Institutions: Please attach a copy of your purchase order. If you have not purchased from Herald House previously, please furnish credit information on the reverse side of this form.

Individuals: Please send check, money order, or credit card information unless you have an established account.

Purchase Order No. _____

Ordered by: _____

Phone _____

Bill to _____

Address _____

City _____

State _____ Zip _____

Visa or Mastercard Number _____

Expiration _____

Call toll-free 1-800-821-7550, Missouri residents call 1-800-346-3026 x387